Kisses of Sunshine
for Grandmas

Also by Gracie Malone
in Large Print:

Still Making Waves

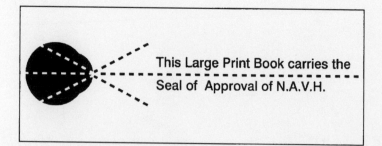

This Large Print Book carries the
Seal of Approval of N.A.V.H.

Carol Kent and Gracie Malone

Kisses of Sunshine for Grandmas

Thorndike Press • Waterville, Maine

The website addresses recommended are offered as a resource to you. These websites are not intended in any way to be or imply an endorsement on the part of Zondervan, nor do we vouch for their content for the life of this book.

Published in 2006 by arrangement with The Zondervan Corporation LLC.

Thorndike Press® Large Print Christian Living.

The tree indicium is a trademark of Thorndike Press.

The text of this Large Print edition is unabridged. Other aspects of the book may vary from the original edition.

Set in 16 pt. Plantin by Al Chase.

Printed in the United States on permanent paper.

Library of Congress Cataloging-in-Publication Data

Kisses of sunshine for grandmas / [edited] by Carol Kent and Gracie Malone.
    p. cm. — (Thorndike Press large print Christian living)
    ISBN 0-7862-8446-3 (lg. print : hc : alk. paper)
    1. Grandmothers — Prayer-books and devotions — English. 2. Grandmothers — Anecdotes. 3. Large type books. I. Kent, Carol, 1947– II. Malone, Gracie. III. Thorndike Press large print Christian living series.
BV4847.K57 2006
242′.6431—dc22   2005033427

To Luke, Connor, Mary Catherine,
Abby, Montana, and Myles

Gracie Malone

To Chelsea and Hannah

Carol Kent

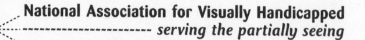
National Association for Visually Handicapped
------------------------- serving the partially seeing

As the Founder/CEO of NAVH, the only national health agency solely devoted to those who, although not totally blind, have an eye disease which could lead to serious visual impairment, I am pleased to recognize Thorndike Press* as one of the leading publishers in the large print field.

Founded in 1954 in San Francisco to prepare large print textbooks for partially seeing children, NAVH became the pioneer and standard setting agency in the preparation of large type.

Today, those publishers who meet our standards carry the prestigious "Seal of Approval" indicating high quality large print. We are delighted that Thorndike Press is one of the publishers whose titles meet these standards. We are also pleased to recognize the significant contribution Thorndike Press is making in this important and growing field.

Lorraine H. Marchi, L.H.D.
Founder/CEO
NAVH

* Thorndike Press encompasses the following imprints: Thorndike, Wheeler, Walker and Large Print Press.

contents

introduction

This *Kisses of Sunshine* series of five books — one each for grandmas, moms, sisters, teachers, and women — has lighthearted, uplifting, often humorous stories meant to bring a sunburst of joy to your life — as you remember that God loves you. Gracie Malone has joined me in putting these stories together, and our purpose is simply to let God's love so warm and fill you that you become warmth, light, and love to a cold, dark world.

Theresa Bloomingdale once said, "If your baby is beautiful and perfect, never cries or fusses, sleeps on schedule and burps on demand, an angel all the time — you're the grandma." On a personal note, there is nothing that brings me more pleasure than spending time with my granddaughters. I have their pictures in my wallet and their drawings on my refrigerator. I pray for them every day and envision what they might "be" when they grow up.

Having taught speech and drama, I look forward to their dramatic productions where I become "an audience of one," applauding their dramatic puppet shows and cheering after their living room musical productions. I think Chelsea and Hannah are as close to "professional actresses" as children can be, and I am convinced their IQs are higher than most elementary school kids.

Yes, I'm prejudiced, because I am a grandma — and that gives me every right to brag, exaggerate, and overstate their accomplishments. I know they are the best, the smartest, the most well behaved, the prettiest, and the most charming of all children. I should know — they're *mine!*

The coauthor of this book is Gracie Malone. If her name sounds familiar, it's because she's an expert in the art of grandparenting and her book *Off My Rocker* is a favorite of grandparents everywhere. Gracie has more stories than almost anyone I know, and she tells them in a manner that makes me grab my stomach because I'm laughing so hard I can hardly sit still while I'm reading. Gracie is not only funny, she's filled with wisdom, love, and compassion. You'll get to know Grandma Gracie very personally as you read this book — and you'll be a better grandma, too, because her techniques work. Both of us deeply appreciate our gifted editor, Sandra Vander Zicht, and the creative team at Zondervan for giving us the privilege of working on such a delightful project.

I'm also grateful to the remarkable women who shared their own grandparenting stories in this book. You made me laugh and cry — and you reminded me that I don't have to be perfect to be a good grandma. William James once said, "The great use of life is to spend it on something that will outlast it." I'm spending my life investing time in my grandchildren. I hope this book will inspire you to do the same.

— Carol Kent, General Editor

my children's children

Gracie Malone

*Before you were conceived I wanted you.
Before you were born I loved you.
Before you were here one hour I would
die for you.*

Maureen Hawkins

One morning our oldest son, Matt, called
with the news I'd been waiting for. "If you
hurry," he blurted out, "you can make it for
the birth of your grandson." I jumped in the
car and headed for the hospital. The drive
from our hometown of Greenville to theirs
in Carrollton would take almost an hour.
On the way, my heart beat at a faster-than-
usual pace as I thought about the new baby
as well as the new role my children would be
assuming. It was fun to imagine Matt as a
daddy and Rebecca as a mom. I knew they
would be good parents. And I couldn't wait
to meet the newest member of our clan.

I whipped into a parking place, pushed through the front door of Trinity Medical Center, and headed down the hall toward the maternity wing. Rounding the corner into the waiting room, I spotted Matt dressed in hospital scrubs, a surgical mask hanging loosely around his neck. Apparently the childbirth classes had prepared him to be a fully participating member of the delivery team.

With a broad sweep of his hand he motioned me onward. "Follow me!" Pushing through the swinging doors, he escorted me down the hall and into the birthing room.

Rebecca was nestled in a contraption that looked more like Joe's recliner than a hospital bed. She looked tired, but, to my surprise, was fully awake and smiling as she extended a tiny bundle in my direction. "Want to hold him?" she asked.

Yes! Of course I did.

I gently took Baby Luke from his mother's arms and pulled him close to my bosom. He was only minutes old. The tiny little boy felt warm as he wiggled and stretched. I'd forgotten how small a newborn baby is, barely big enough to fit in the crook of a woman's arm. As I gazed into his slate blue eyes, straining to focus in the soft light, I was suddenly overcome with emotion — the same feelings I'd experienced when I held my own newborn sons — love, joy, hope, and a swelling sense of pride. I swallowed hard, choking back the lump rising in my throat.

My eyes examined the features of my newborn grandson — a perfect heart-shaped mouth, tiny upturned nose, a slight crimp on both ears. I folded back the corner of the blue flannel blanket that swaddled him and touched his hand. When four tiny wrinkled fingers curled around one of my own, I knew I was hooked for life. I blinked back a tear as I marveled at the wonder of God's creation.

I remembered a verse from Psalms describing a developing baby as "intricately and curiously wrought [as if embroidered with various colors]" (Psalm 139:15, Amplified Bible). The thought that God, the awesome Creator of the universe, had been "intricately" involved in the design of my precious grandson brought tears of joy to my eyes.

I lifted the tiny bundle close to my lips and whispered against the soft folds of skin, "Luke, I'm your grandmother. I love you. I always will, no matter what."

With the birth of this little boy, our family had come full circle, making our own revolution in the great circle of life. A new generation was born that day — one that would bear our name.

Since the birth of Luke, I've been in the waiting room during the arrival of five additional grandchildren. Luke was barely three when his parents presented him with a little brother, Connor. They in turn welcomed two little sisters, Mary Catherine and Abby. Our son Mike and daughter-in-law Jeanna blessed us with two little boys — Montana and Myles.

Each child came into the world with unique features, characteristics, and temperaments. And with the birth of each child, the promise of a brighter future and hope for tomorrow was reborn in my heart.

Whenever I hold a newborn grandchild in my arms, why, I feel newborn myself.

You made all the delicate inner parts of my body and knit me together in my mother's womb. Thank you for making me so wonderfully complex! Your workmanship is marvelous — and how well I know it.
Psalm 139:13–14 NLT

terms of endearment

Gracie Malone

*I don't care what you call me;
just call me.*

Anonymous

When our grandson Luke started babbling, all ears perked up. "Dah-d-d-d-dah, M-m-m-m-m, Mah!" Eventually the jabbered syllables became words — the ones he would use to identify his parents. Little Luke didn't say the usual toddler words, "Dada" or "Mama." Oh, no! One day while munching on a handful of Cheerios, he nonchalantly looked up at my daughter-in-law and addressed her in a very grown-up manner as "Mom." A few days later he pronounced my son's long-sought "Dad." We were elated. After two years of parental coaxing, Luke could talk. Now, I wondered, what would he call me?

My mother is "Me Ma" — a name lovingly bestowed on her by grandson number one. My friend Carol is "Mia." I know one "Mimi," two "Grams" and a "G-mother." One of my friends is addressed with the very British sounding "Grandma-ma." My sister Lois is identified by the conventional title "Grandmother." Even the youngest of her grandkids is able to mouth the distinguished sounding term. Lois is delighted. In her opinion, *grandmother* is "the most beautiful word a grandchild can say."

One afternoon Lois explained how the grandmother titling process works. "You see," she began, "it's Luke's choice. No matter what you call yourself, he will make his own selection and, most likely, your future grandchildren will follow suit. Don't worry about it, Gracie. Whatever he calls you, I'm sure it will be just perfect." With that bit of information safely tucked away in my memory bank, I waited and I wondered.

Then one day, just as Lois predicted, when I was stacking blocks with Luke, it happened. He placed his block atop the leaning tower we'd built on my living room floor, grinned, and started to speak, "Gr-r-r-r." My heart skipped a beat as I waited for the word "gr-r-r-andma" or "gr-r-r-andmother" to come from his peanut-butter-covered mouth. But his enunciation was perfectly clear as he said, "Gr-r-r-acie."

I have to admit I was a bit disappointed. I had hoped to have my grandchildren call me something more tender and, well . . . unique and special, maybe even something classy or cute. Nevertheless, I was delighted that my grandson had spoken my name. And I thought perhaps my title would change as Luke's verbal skills developed; maybe it would even evolve into something a little more traditional.

It didn't happen.

Even when his parents coaxed and made suggestions, my moniker stuck like a piece of gum on the bottom of my shoe. "Gr-r-racie," Luke would bellow, and, in spite of feeling a bit chagrined at the grown-up manner the little tyke spoke my name, I'd come-a-runnin'.

Gracie is what Luke called me until his parents finally convinced him to add the title "Grandma." It just seemed the respectable thing to do. So today I am Luke's "Grandma Gracie." (I'm also "Grandma Gracie" to a whole passel of subsequent grandchildren.)

And I've decided my sister was right after all. "Grandma Gracie" was the perfect choice. In spite of the fifty-year age gap between us, my grandson and I have a "Luke

and Gracie" kind of relationship. A friendship — one I will cherish for the rest of my
days.

*A good name is to be more desired than
great wealth,
Favor is better than silver and gold.*
Proverbs 22:1 NASB

a tale of two angels

Carol Kent

*Nobody can do for little children
what grandparents do.
Grandparents sort of sprinkle stardust
over the lives of little children.*

Alex Haley

The day had been exhilarating. I was speaking at an arena event in Denver and called home for messages. Our son, a recent graduate of the U.S. Naval Academy, was in nuclear engineering school in Orlando, Florida. His voice mail communication was short: "Mom and Dad, some things are comin' down. We have to talk." Click.

When we got through to Jason several hours later, he picked up where he left off: "My naval orders have changed. I have to be at Surface Warfare Officers' School in Newport, Rhode Island, on September 8. April and I are in love and we want to get married next Friday."

My heart leaped as I realized what I had just heard:

My son was asking to marry a woman I had never met *next Friday!*

He was also telling me he was going to marry a previously married woman with *two children* next Friday!

I was having trouble breathing, let alone talking, so my husband carried on the conversation as I dialogued with God:

> Hello, God? Do you remember me? I've been praying for my son's future wife since he was in my womb. Lord, did you hear those prayers? Do you remember I asked you for a virgin? This woman does not qualify!

Rational thinking returned slowly. We asked Jason and his new fiancée if they would wait three weeks and be married in our hometown with the accountability of family and friends around them. They agreed.

A week and a half later Jason and April walked through our front door with their arms encircled around each other's waists. It didn't take me long to love April. She had been married at the age of sixteen to a man ten years her senior and she had been through more of "the tough stuff of life" than anyone deserves in this lifetime.

Behind the two of them, in walked six-year-old Chelsea and three-year-old Hannah. Within a half hour, little Chelsea came running up to me. She took my hand in her two hands, made serious eye contact with me, and said, "You're my new favorite Grammy!" My heart melted.

Every morning Hannah burst out of her bedroom with exuberant enthusiasm. She sat on a stool at my kitchen breakfast bar and ate her cereal, singing between every bite: "I love Jesus; he loves me! I love Jesus; he loves me!" These precious little girls had won my heart within hours.

For the next week and a half I enjoyed all of the fun of being an "instant Grammy" as we prepared for the wedding. Chelsea and Hannah had full access to my closet and they dressed up in chiffon and long beads. My two little angels danced and sang whenever they heard music in the back-ground:

- "Grammy, can I please put on some of your makeup?"
- "Oh-h-h-h-h! Look at this dress! It

has a flow-ee skirt. May I please wear it?"
- "I found Grammy's high heels! They are so-o-o beautiful. I'm going to look like a princess!"
- "Pleeeeze, Grammy, can we fill your bathtub with bubbles and go swimming?"
- "Do we *have* to go to bed? Please read us a story."

As the wedding day approached, I saw the deep love in the eyes of my son and his bride. And I already loved my big-brown-eyed granddaughters. I wasn't there for their births, but they were filling my heart with so much joy. Two little angels entered my life at an unexpected time and showered me with unconditional love and acceptance. I had a new name — *Grammy!* And I had a new passion — to be a godly influence in the lives of my granddaughters.

God *did* answer my prayer. But the answer came in a different package than I was expecting.

You're blessed when you stay on course, walking steadily on the road revealed by God.
Psalm 119:1 MSG

the magical white sword

Heidi McLaughlin

*Anything large enough
for a wish to light upon
is large enough to hang a prayer on.*

George MacDonald

When my grandson Alex was three years old, he loved swords. Of course, his parents would not buy him one, but he improvised with anything he could find — a stick, a creatively constructed Lego, or a wooden spoon. Alex is the middle child in a family of three energetic boys, and even though he was the quiet one, he had a way of tugging at my heart. When the boys came to visit us that summer, I promised all three of them a trip to an adventure park. As soon as they arrived, Alex jumped out of the van and ran to me. He looked at me with his big eyes and said, "Nana, when can we go to Old Mac-Donald's Farm?"

Saturday morning arrived, and we were on our way. As we walked into the building to buy our tickets, Alex spotted a box on the floor. The box was full of swords of every color, size, and shape — and I could see Alex wanted one. I said to him what every good Nana says, "Alex, if you are a good boy today, I will buy you a sword when we are done." He was perfectly behaved all day.

When our excursion was over, he ran to the sword box, and I could see his little eyes darting back and forth between his two favorites — from the blue sword to the white one. He simply could not decide. One moment it was the blue one, the next moment it was the white one, until he finally said, "Okay, Nana, I'll take the blue one." We made the purchase and headed to the parking lot.

We had not even arrived at the car when he tugged at my hand and said, "Nana, I really want the *white* one." Too late. The blue one had been purchased. He cried all the way home, but even though it broke my heart, I felt he needed to learn early in life the results of making choices.

It was a whole year later that we were visiting his family on Vancouver Island, British Columbia, when I asked Alex if he would like to come along with me to run an errand.

I strapped him into his car seat, and as we were driving down the highway, I heard his little voice shyly admit, "Nana, I really wanted the *white* one!" Our eyes met in the rearview mirror, and I had to look away because tears were welling up in my eyes. If he would have demanded the white sword and whined, it would have been a different story, but what I really heard him saying was, "Nana, you did not hear what was in my heart."

I quietly responded, "Alex, I am so sorry you did not get your white sword."

Many months passed, and I was in the middle of my Christmas shopping when I saw it. A white sword. The most beautiful white sword I had ever seen. It had gold edging, gold tassels, and it had its own case. I bought the sword, took it home, and wrapped it up tenderly for my little Alex. I mailed it in a box with a note for his mommy to please put it under the Christmas tree so Alex could have it on Christmas morning.

I could hardly wait for the report. On Christmas morning his little blue eyes flew wide open as he saw that strange shape under the tree. Between ripping wrapping paper and unabashed giggles, he shouted over and over, "It's my white sword! It's my white sword!" Even at his young age he knew that this gift was not from Santa, but from his Nana.

I wanted him to have his magical white sword. He never demanded it, but in his quiet way he told me the desires of his heart. I wanted him to know his request was significant enough for me to hear.

My love for Alex is a lot like God's love for me. He knows the desires of my heart, and he's just waiting for me to ask so he can grant them.

And how bold and free we then become in his presence, freely asking according to his will, sure that he's listening.

And if we're confident that he's listening, we know that what we've asked for is as good as ours.
1 John 5:14–15 MSG

cheez whiz

Gracie Malone

The happiness of life is made up of minute factors — the little soon-forgotten charities of a kiss or smile, a kind look, a heartfelt compliment.

Samuel Taylor Coleridge

Joe and I had decided to spend Christmas with our son Mike and his family at their house in The Woodlands. It was a break with tradition, but one that would have its own unique charm. Relieved of the duties of being Home Management Specialist in Charge, I was free to enjoy my grandchildren, Montana and Myles, and I spent hours with them playing games, telling stories, and watching Christmas videos.

One evening I gathered the boys on my lap for story time. I had brushed my teeth, showered, dressed in comfy pajamas, and applied a liberal amount of antiwrinkle cream (rather expensive antiwrinkle cream, I might add!) to my freshly cleansed face before meeting them on the sofa.

I'd no sooner settled into the plush cushions when Myles climbed on my lap and hugged me tightly. The little guy's bright blue eyes danced as he took my face in his hands in a gentle caress. Then he patted me softly on both cheeks and whispered, "Mmm, mmm, Gamma Gacie, you smell good! You smell just like a piece of cheese."

I burst out laughing, until the startled look on Myles' upturned face stopped me cold. He grinned and sweetly added, "I *wuv* cheese!"

My heart filled with joy as I pulled the little boy close. What greater compliment could he have given? To him, I smelled good enough to eat!

The next morning we awoke to discover that Santa Claus had indeed come to town, bringing a bag full of toys for the kids and a few gifts for their grandma as well.

Among the bounty, I discovered a beautiful tray made of amber stained glass — a gift to me from our son Jason. Mounted on the tray was an assortment of bath-and-body products labeled "Aroma Therapy." As I removed the clear cellophane wrapper, I found myself wondering what actual therapeutic effect an "aroma" could have on a person. What kind of smell could alter my mood?

Reading from the label, I saw that Jason had selected "orange ginger." I couldn't wait to give the lotion the sniff test. It smelled good! Strong citrus overtones with just a hint of pungent ginger.

The next day I gave the products a thorough analysis. I soaked my body in a tub of hot water seasoned with bubble bath, scrubbed my feet with granulated gel, and anointed my skin with lotion. Later, as I settled under the blankets on my bed, I realized the products had indeed lived up to their therapeutic claims. I was completely relaxed without a care in the world.

Except maybe for one.

I kept wondering if Myles would be equally enamored with a grandmother who smelled like a piece of fruit instead of his favorite cheese.

As I drifted off to sleep, the scent of orange ginger wafted up to my nostrils and my thoughts took on a heavenly perspective. I remembered something written long before high-tech sales gimmicks and media hype influenced our fragrance choices — words that describe an "aromatherapy" of the spirit. Seems there is one fragrance that cannot only warm a person's heart, it can literally change the world — the aroma of Christ.

Thanks be to God, who always leads us in triumphal procession in Christ and through us spreads everywhere the fragrance of the knowledge of him. For we are to God the aroma of Christ among those who are being saved.
2 Corinthians 2:14–15

time for a change

Gracie Malone

We may give without loving,
but we cannot love without giving.

Robert Louis Stevenson

To celebrate their anniversary, our son
Matt and daughter-in-law Rebecca planned
an overnight trip, and we volunteered to
keep our eighteen-month-old grandson,
Luke. His parents had warned me that because of the little toddler's boundless
energy, even a simple task like changing his
diaper would not be easy.

As luck would have it, even before his parents escaped through the front door, my
sensitive olfactory nerve alerted me that
Luke needed changing. Wanting to impress
Matt with my grandparenting skills, I
grabbed a fresh "Huggie" and cornered
Luke at the top of the stairs.

I'd no sooner popped the gripper snaps

on his overalls than I realized this job was more than I'd bargained for. Luke was a mess! Besides that, he was in a playful mood. He pivoted sideways, grabbed his tennis shoes, and began trying to untie the laces. I made a funny face and then I tried to distract him with a quick story. Luke wiggled and squirmed. After a few anxious minutes, I did what any out-of-practice grandmother would do — I yelled for help.

Papa Joe bounded up the stairs and tried to distract Luke from the activity taking place on his lower extremities by playfully pinning his shoulders to the floor like a wrestling pro, complete with appropriate grunts and snorts. Luke kicked and giggled in response. I grabbed his legs and began the cleanup operation.

Before long, I realized that in my haste I'd forgotten one important diaper-changing component — the Chubby Wipes. I had no choice but to involve our teenaged son. "Jason," I bellowed, "bring me the wipes from the diaper bag!" He brought them promptly, extending the package with one hand while holding his nose with the other.

Then, just as I thought I had everything under control, Luke dirtied the clean diaper and I had to start all over again.

"Matt," I yelled, "before you go, could

you bring me another diaper!"

When Matt rounded the corner, clean diaper in hand, he shook his head in disbelief. "I refuse to be part of a four-man pit crew." He let out a devilish cackle as he headed for his car, his voice trailing off as he ran, "You are now the official adults in charge. Good luck, you guys!"

Since the aforementioned babysitting experience with our first grandchild, I've had many more opportunities to take care of our little ones, and my confidence has grown. Today, with a half dozen little ones vying for my attention, overnight visits and just-for-fun sleepovers are frequent occurrences. And whenever the kids come over, my child-care skills that had been highly developed as a mother come back to my aging mind with vivid clarity. In addition, I have an overwhelming love for my grandchildren — the kind of love that makes even the yukkiest job seem not so bad after all.

God can pour on the blessings in astonishing ways so that you're ready for anything and everything, more than just ready to do what needs to be done.
2 Corinthians 9:8 MSG

through the eyes
of grace

Debi Stack

*Love is a fruit in season at all times,
and within reach of every hand.*

Mother Teresa

I don't know which was heavier — the ripped grocery sack that held all my end-of-fifth-grade stuff or my heart that held another day's worth of cruel words from my classmates. Shuffling off the school bus as it stopped at my house, I resigned myself to another miserable afternoon and a long, lonely summer.

Just then a familiar sound changed everything. From my front porch rang a cheery greeting: "There's our girl!" I looked up, then ran — grinning — to the open arms of Grandma Grace. Tall and well-groomed, Grandma Grace had a natural aristocratic air that matched her regal profile. But her grand exterior belied her most endearing qualities — down-to-earth faith, an affectionate nature, and constant good humor. A beloved family friend since before I was born, she sometimes stayed with me while my parents worked. We adored her.

Aptly named, Grace Darling had a joyful outlook on life. It sparkled from her eyes; it shone in her smile; it seasoned her speech with genuine kindness. This was a woman who created reasons to celebrate. Who else would phone us out of the blue to say, "I just paid my bills — let's have a picnic!" She maintained her deportment even while teaching me, between bouts of laughter, how to rise from lying on the floor with a cup of water balanced on my forehead. But on this day, because I had been expecting to enter an empty house, her presence especially delighted me.

"Come on in. Don't you look pretty? How about a treat?" Grandma Grace hugged me tightly, then led the way to the kitchen. I leaned against the counter next to her, mesmerized at how she peeled an enormous apple with a single, springy strip. After quartering and seeding it, she sliced . . . and sliced . . . and sliced . . . until no slice could possibly be sliced again.

At last, paper-thin pieces of succulent apple towered in my bowl. Lifting it to the kitchen window and turning it slowly, I watched the color-changing play of sunlight upon the translucent slices — snowy white, cool ivory, flawless cream, or the palest glowing gold I'd ever seen. Yes, these were the same apples that I chomped right out of my hand on most days, but somehow, when Grandma Grace prepared them, they tasted like a delicacy fit for a princess.

Maybe that's because as she sliced the apple, Grandma Grace visited with me as if I were the most fascinating person in the world. She *looked* at me when I talked — always smiling — and never failed to interject generous compliments. When I groaned that boys didn't like tall brainy girls like me, she replied, "But haven't you noticed that all the Miss Americas are tall and smart like you? *You* could be Miss America someday!"

Since then, apples have always reminded me of Grandma Grace. In her hands, this simple snack became something extraordinary. The glistening crescents of fruit — slice after slice after slice — showed I was *worth* the extra effort and filled my empty bowl. But sweeter still were the simple words from Grandma Grace herself — word after word after word that filled my aching heart:

"You are beautiful."
"You are special."
"You are talented."
"You are important."
"You are loved."

Grandma Grace passed away soon after I graduated from college, but during the lonely years of my girlhood, and even through some of the hard times in my adult life, I have often recalled her spirit-nourishing words. Time has not lessened their sweetness, nor is my heart ever filled to less than overflowing.

A word aptly spoken is like apples of gold in settings of silver.
Proverbs 25:11

great grandkid quips

Gracie Malone

Lettin' the cat outta the bag is a whole lot easier 'n puttin' it back in.

Will Rogers

One bright morning an aged grandfather and his four-year-old granddaughter were sitting on the front porch talking. As children her age are prone to do, she began probing him with questions.

"Did God make you, Grandpa?"

"Of course God made me," the grandfather answered.

After a moment, the child said, "Did God make me too?"

"He sure did," the man answered. He couldn't hold back a proud grin as he looked into her bright blue eyes and noticed her tiny legs twirling in circles as they dangled from the too tall wicker chair.

For several minutes, the little girl seemed

to be studying her grandpa as well as her own reflection in the window. He wondered what was running through her mind. At last she spoke up, "You know, Grandpa, God's doing a lot better job lately."

Our son Mike and his buddy Tommy were both four when their inquisitive little minds got them into a heap of trouble. All day long they'd watched from Tommy's backyard as movers unloaded a huge van parked in front of the vacant house next door. As the men tugged on furniture and rolled appliances into the house, Tommy and Mike became more and more curious about the new neighbors. Finally a friendly looking lady came out the back door. The boys jumped out of the sandbox and ran to the chain link fence that separated the backyards. In typical preschool fashion, they struck up a conversation.

"What's your name?" Tommy began.

The lady smiled. "I'm Mrs. Frawley."

Like two kid-sized lawyers they put their heads together for a small conference. Then Tommy took a deep breath and fired off another question — the most important question of all.

"Do you have any little boys in the house?"

"No," Mrs. Frawley answered.

The boys were visibly disappointed. Nevertheless, after a few moments, Mike continued the inquisition where Tommy had left off. "Do you have any little girls in the house?"

"No, I don't," she answered patiently.

Tommy turned his hands palms up, looked at Mike, then back to Mrs. Frawley. "Do you have a baby in the house?"

"No!" Looking a bit perturbed, the new neighbor turned to go back inside.

By this time Tommy was completely frustrated. How could a mommy and daddy not have children? And, more specifically, how could the people moving in next door not have kids for Mike and him to play with? As Mrs. Frawley made her way toward her back door, he shouted, "Well, do you have any babies in your tummy?"

"Where do babies come from?" is one question that has universal interest for deep-thinking four-year-olds. And when the topic comes up, it causes many a mother or grandmother to catch her breath and pray for wisdom. The question surfaced at our house one day as I sat on the floor playing with our grandkids — five-year-old Mary Catherine and eight-year-old Connor.

Mary was rearranging the dress on her Barbie doll when out of the blue she said, "I don't know how a girl can have a baby when she's not married." I fumbled with a tiny pair of Barbie's high heels and waited, hoping one of her parents had overheard the conversation and would come to my rescue. No such luck. I was still trying to formulate an answer when Connor spoke up.

"Oh, Mary." He twisted his lips into a crooked smirk and quipped, "Don't you know anything? You adopt!"

I praise you, Father, Lord of heaven and earth, because you have hidden these things from the wise and learned, and revealed them to little children.
Matthew 11:25

the birthday gift

Ginger Shaw

Kids are smart, you know,
and they know what's going on.
You're not fooling them a bit.
They know you're bewildered and
confused and don't know all the answers,
and they know
that the louder you say something
the less sure you are that it is right.

Bob Benson

The package arrived in time for my thirteenth birthday. Small, simply wrapped, it was sent from Nana, my paternal grandmother in California. We seldom saw Nana or heard from her, but she always sent birthday and Christmas gifts. And she gave great gifts. Not expensive, not fun toys, but real "lady" gifts: silk stockings, gloves, and beautiful slips. As I removed the brown paper and the flowered wrapping tissue, my eyes fell upon a small white leather Bible with my name embossed in gold on the front cover. A beautiful, small, elegant Bible — just like the one my older sister had received on her thirteenth birthday. The gift made me feel mature and grown up.

I knew this was an important gift, a real coming-of-age present. What I didn't understand is why Nana sent me a Bible. I had never seen her go to church, never heard her talk about God, and I never heard her mention any story from that book. Oh, there was an old large Bible on a table in her living room. But with the exception of births and marriages written in the front, it appeared unread, unused, and untouched. And the few times I had ventured to look inside that book, I was reminded it was to be left untouched.

I had missed growing up around my grandmothers and had never known my grandfathers. The times we visited my maternal grandmother, I remember walking to church with her on Sunday mornings when most of the family slept. I remember, too, talking with her about all the stories I had heard in Sunday school and church. Her simple answers, kind nature, and gentle wisdom taught me much of what it meant to be a Christian.

47

That year I experienced a personal relationship with God through faith in Jesus Christ. It meant a lot to me, but I have never understood what it meant to my grandmother. I wondered if she simply thought of faith as a religious tradition.

We were three thousand miles away from Nana, so I sent the obligatory thank-you note. I couldn't ask her in person why she sent me a Bible or what it meant to her. And I'm not sure I would have asked her. Never once do I remember her sharing a personal memory or story. Perhaps it was just her generation or just her personality. Nana didn't talk about herself; she gave instruction and correction.

Over the years I wondered about the meaning of that gift. I tried to understand a woman I never really knew. I tried to excuse her "closed" personality to distance, circumstances, past pain. But then I thought of my other grandmother, who leaped tall mountains to be with us whenever possible. She opened her heart and mind and let me look inside the pages of her life. We both are richer for her openness.

In retrospect, both my grandmothers taught me the same lesson: you really *can't* tell a book by its cover. It is the life lived as an open book that is the greater gift. I intend to live an "open book life" and leave the story of God's work in my life for future generations.

You yourselves are our letter, written on our hearts, known and read by everybody. You show that you are a letter from Christ, the result of our ministry, written not with ink but with the Spirit of the living God, not on tablets of stone but on tablets of human hearts.
2 Corinthians 3:2–3

the greatest cheerleader

Shari Minke

Grandmas are moms with lots of frosting.

Anonymous

"Mom!" my new stepson shouted. "Grandma wants to talk to you!"

Picking up the phone, I said, "Hi, Dorothy; how are you?"

"Fine, dear, and how are you doing?" I internalized that she called me "dear."

After the usual small talk, I risked asking, "Dorothy, may I ask you a personal question?"

"Sure," she said spontaneously.

"Recently I was talking with the mother of my friend Sandy. Sandy died of cancer, leaving two little boys behind, just like your daughter, Nancy, did. Sandy's mother, Betty, told me that when her son-in-law remarried, it was difficult for her to hear her grandsons call another woman 'Mom.'

Betty thought you may be having some of those same feelings. I never thought of how hard it might be for you when you hear Doug and Scott call me 'Mom.' Is that painful for you?"

There was a pause. "Yes, dear, to be honest, it does hurt. But I want you to know it has nothing to do with you. What is painful is that Dad and I miss our Nancy, and we always will. Even though it hurts to hear the boys call you 'Mom,' we wouldn't want it any other way. We love you and we're glad you're the mother of our grand-sons. We don't always understand God's plans, but we believe that now God wants *you* to be the mother of Doug and Scott."

Many months later, Dorothy told me, "Just before you and Tom were married, Dad and I intentionally moved to Florida to live for a few months, hoping the boys would bond more quickly to you if we weren't around."

The love and sacrifice of these precious grandparents was astounding!

While Grandma and Grandpa were in Florida, every two weeks on Sunday morning, the boys ran to the phone to talk with them. During the time their daughter, Nancy, was fighting her battle with leukemia, they had been the primary caregivers to their grandsons. That resulted in a very close relationship between the boys and Nancy's parents. Doug and Scott smothered Grandma and Grandpa with hugs and kisses when they arrived back in Michigan to live.

At Doug and Scott's T-ball and baseball games or any other sports activities, Grandma rose to her full stature of four feet, ten inches, clapping and cheering, "Go, Scott! . . . Go, Doug! . . . Yea! . . . Good job!"

One warm summer night while sitting on the bleachers, Dorothy confided to me, "Before Nancy died, I promised that on her behalf, I would yell the loudest for the boys to cheer them on." Tears welled up in my eyes.

As Mother's Day approached, my heart was filled with appreciation for this remarkable woman. In the letter I tucked in her card, I expressed these thoughts:

Dear Dorothy,

Without you and Lefty, there would have been no Nancy. Through your love, Nancy was born and blessed many lives, mine included.

In two days our country will celebrate Mother's Day. I wanted to write you because I want you to know that in my heart I honor you and Nancy.

Two weeks ago I was touched deeply that you introduced me as your "daughter-in-law." From the first time I met you, you have given me unconditional love and acceptance. You have always been an encourager and a support.

While I call you "Dorothy" to your face, in my heart I call you "Mom."

I am thankful you and I have been able to talk openly through the years. I thank you for cheering for the boys all these years on Nancy's behalf at the T-ball, soccer, baseball, football, and basketball games. Nancy would be so proud of you for keeping your promise to shout the loudest! Bless you for your commitment to her and the boys.

On this Mother's Day I honor you both for the excellent Jesus-focused lives you have lived. God is saying to you both, "Well done, good and faithful servants."

Loving you oh so much,
Shari

Love . . . is not self-seeking, . . . It always protects, always trusts, always hopes, always perseveres.
1 Corinthians 13:4–5, 7

overcoming "g-force" and other free falls

Luke and Gracie Malone

*You know you're getting old
when you get the same sensation
from a rocking chair
that you once got from a roller coaster.*

**"Random Thoughts"
from *FunOne.com***

I don't know what possessed me to say yes. Perhaps I wanted to be considered the world's coolest grandma. Or maybe I did it to satisfy my curiosity. But I really think I just wanted to prove something to myself. After all, who wants to think they're too old or out of shape to keep up with the youngsters or too chicken to try something new?

No matter what motivated me to choose such a course of action, once the decision was made there was no turning back. I fell in line with my twelve-year-old grandson, Luke. I was going to ride "G-Force!"

(There were so many kids pressed into the narrow spaces set aside for the waiting lines, I couldn't have turned back if I'd wanted to. Besides, I was way too cool to admit I was scared spitless.) As we waited our turn, I tried to maintain a calm outward appearance even though my aging knees were knocking uncontrollably and my insides were in a knot.

The following is Luke's version of what happened:

"Since my grandmother is always telling stories about me, I think it's my turn to tell one about her. One year around Christmastime my dad's company had a party, which included a trip to Six Flags Over Texas. When our family got inside the park we decided to get into separate groups and do our own thing.

"My dad and stepmom, Rachel, took Mary, Abby, and Ingrid to the merry-go-round and Papa Joe took Connor and Lexi to ride the Runaway Mine Train. That left Grandma Gracie and me to formulate our own little plan. Suddenly I had an idea. I challenged her to ride the G-Force. It's like an elevator with seats inside. It goes straight up about a hundred feet, then plummets to the ground fast enough to put your stomach in your mouth. Although a little nervous,

Grandma Gracie accepted my offer. We had to wait in line for almost an hour, and the whole time I was telling her stories about how fast and scary the ride was. By the time it was our turn, I had told her so much she was already feeling sick to her stomach.

"Once we got on the ride, they buckled us in, and we started our climb toward the top. Grandma Gracie braced herself by pushing against the front of the elevator with her tennis shoes. Of course I was reassuring her the whole time by saying how the cars don't come off the track that often and as far as I knew, nobody had ever died on this ride.

"Suddenly the car stopped, lurched forward, and I saw a look of sheer terror cross my grandma's face. Then we dropped at a blinding fast speed and, before we knew it, we were on the ground. Although the ride was quick, it still rattled my grandma pretty bad. Shaking knees and all, she hobbled off the ride and headed for the ladies room. I heard her mutter under her breath, 'So that's what g-force means.' "

Having overcome the force of gravity, I must have felt invincible, for when the family got back together, I stood in line with the gang for two or three more gut-wrenching, heart-stopping rides. Before we left the park, I got to choose the last ride. The whole family joined me on my personal favorite — the carousel. Seated on the back of that horse, I breathed a prayer of thanksgiving, for my heavenly Father had been working overtime to keep me safe.

Do not fear, for I am with you; do not be dismayed, for I am your God. I will strengthen you and help you; I will uphold you with my righteous right hand.
Isaiah 41:10

grandma
to the rescue!

Carol Kent

That's it! I'm calling Grandma!

On a T-shirt
worn by an eight-year-old

It happened at breakfast.

Our son was spending a few days with his grandparents in the Upper Peninsula of Michigan. He had enjoyed several fun-packed days of high adventure in the great outdoors. The woods on the property provided a creative outlet for his imaginative ideas for finding hiding places and building forts, and for discovering a wide variety of northern Michigan wildlife. Deer grazed in the front yard and wild turkeys could be seen walking across the gravel road. Robins, blue jays, finches, and sparrows took turns resting on the railing of the rambling old deck as they helped themselves to Grandma's generous offerings of seeds, grain, and fresh water.

One thing everyone knows is that when you visit Grandma's house, you eat well. She is a remarkable cook, and to this day she takes delight in pleasing the palates of her guests — no matter how young they are. Grandchildren are her favorites.

On the morning in question, Grandpa helped with the preparation of breakfast. He opened an old Mason jar of canned prunes and carefully filled three cereal bowls with an ample helping of the contents. He then covered the wrinkled fruit with the prune juice that was left in the jar before placing the bowls at each place setting.

Jason was called for breakfast and sat down at the table. The three of them joined hands and Grandpa asked the blessing in his deepest and most authoritative voice. Following the "Amen," it was time to eat. Grandma had prepared eggs (sunny-side up), farm fresh sausage, and whole wheat toast. She also made breakfast potatoes that had been sliced and fried. And there were prunes — lots of prunes.

Jason dived into the eggs, sausage, potatoes, and toast, but he hadn't touched the prunes. Grandpa observed his reluctance to begin eating the brownish bowl of squishy fruit and announced, "Jason, if you want to keep your 'plumbing' working properly, you'll have to eat a few prunes in your lifetime. They're good for the constitution, and besides, we don't waste anything around here. Eat your prunes, son."

Jason loved his grandfather, and he had always been an obedient child. However, even the sight or smell of prunes caused his stomach to rumble. He gripped his spoon, picked up a prune, and placed it in his mouth. Gagging, he managed to get it down and spit the pit into his spoon. Again and again he dipped the spoon into the bowl and repeated this procedure until the fruit finally disappeared.

Grandpa then said, "Jason, the juice is just as good for you as the prunes, so why don't you empty that bowl, son?"

Jason gazed up at his grandma with a pleading look of desperation while fighting the urge to regurgitate. Suddenly Grandma said, "Clyde, I forgot to get the chicken out of the freezer in time to thaw for tonight's supper. Would you go downstairs and take care of that before I forget?"

Grandpa stood up and went down the basement steps to the freezer. At that moment, Grandma stood to her feet, picked up Jason's bowl of prune juice, and without a word, dumped it down the drain of the kitchen sink. Moving fast, she placed the empty bowl back in front of Jason.

Grandpa emerged from the basement, chicken in hand. Placing it on the counter, he looked over at Jason's empty bowl of prune juice and said, "Now that wasn't so bad after all, was it?"

Jason's eyes locked with Grandma's, and they shared a moment of relief, humor, and a never-to-be-forgotten memory-making moment of reprieve. Grandma had rescued her grandson. The secret was theirs, and it bonded them forever.

Eventually Grandpa heard the true story of what happened that morning, and the entire family laughs out loud as the story is repeated, complete with a few exaggerations. One thing is certain. As we make our memories and share our stories, we are weaving laughter, connection, and meaning into the fiber of our relationships with the next generation.

A twinkle in the eye means joy in the heart.
Proverbs 15:30 MSG

strictly a female female

Gracie Malone

When I have a brand new hair-do,
with my eyelashes all in curl,
I float as the clouds on air do —
I enjoy being a girl!

Rodgers and Hammerstein

As soon as we heard the results of my daughter-in-law's prenatal sonogram, I was beside myself with sheer joy. The new addition was a girl! Being the mother of three sons and a grandmother to two incredible little boys, I'd had my share of "hammers 'n nails 'n puppy dog tails." I was ready for some "sugar and spice" — and ribbons and lace and frilly pink dresses. For the next few months, we planned and prayed and stock-piled some of the aforementioned girly things. While we waited, her parents se-lected a girly-girl name: Mary Catherine.

When the day of her delivery finally arrived, Joe and I, along with our teenaged son, Jason, jumped in the car and headed to the hospital where we met the excited young family in the waiting room. As the drama of Mary Catherine's birth unfolded, we each handled the blessed event in our own unique way.

Connor, Mary Catherine's three-year-old brother, had come to the hospital well prepared — bearing a backpack strapped to his tiny shoulders. It literally bulged with toy cars, a few favorite books, and a generous supply of fruit and cookies. He pulled up a chair at the kid-sized table in the middle of the waiting room, opened a Ziplock bag, and began consoling himself with food. (I can really relate to this kid. I was munching on crackers and sipping hot coffee.)

Finally his daddy pushed through the double doors leading to the delivery wing and presented us with the news of Mary Catherine's birth. Connor was overwhelmed and feelings of jealousy seemed to be playing about his frazzled little mind. I coaxed him to sit beside me and tried to comfort him. "Connor, now you are a big brother and you can help take care of your baby sister."

He twisted in his chair and a downcast look crossed his face as he muttered, "I don't wanna talk about it."

I was afraid that little Mary Catherine might be in for a rather cool reception until Connor's daddy offered him a special privilege. Extending his hand, Matt asked, "Connor, would you like to be first to visit your mother and baby sister?"

I breathed an audible sigh of relief when, after a few minutes, Connor strutted back into the waiting room and triumphantly announced, "We're gonna keep her."

Confident that Connor had made peace with his "big brother" status, we turned our attention to his five-year-old brother, Luke. He had worried about the birth of his sister in his own predictable style. He had paced the floor like an expectant father, wiping his brow with the back of his hand and holding his tummy. Several times he had asked me, "Grandma Gracie, how do you make a stomach stop hurting?"

Luke experienced a few minutes of relief after the birth — until we gathered at the nursery window to watch the nurse measure, weigh, and diaper the baby. It was fun to watch as the nurse pressed Mary Catherine's tiny feet onto a black inkpad and made footprints on her birth certificate. But then she unwrapped a sterile needle and proceeded to prick Mary Catherine's heel.

As a tiny red drop of blood appeared, Luke slapped his hand on his forehead and moaned, "What is she doing? She made our baby bleed!"

I winked at Joe and whispered, "You reckon there's a blood test for Luke's high-energy Type A personality?"

A few days later baby Mary Catherine went home from the hospital wearing a precious pink outfit with rows of lace stitched on the back, a lace headband around her forehead, and, of all things, lace on her socks. This child was definitely female! It was a reality that Connor would understand better a few days later.

Our daughter-in-law was changing Mary Catherine's diaper as the little guy nonchalantly observed. Suddenly he gasped and, with a flash of insight, said, "Yep, it's a girl." His brow wrinkled as he added, "I think."

He created them male and female and blessed them.
Genesis 5:2

just call me "mud"

Cynthia Spell Humbert

*Joy is a net of love
by which you can catch souls.*

Mother Teresa

If you are looking for the perfect "southern Belle," you need look no further. Picture Scarlet O'Hara in the twenty-first century, but blonde, and five feet, six inches tall. A beautiful package, and yes, she just happens to be my mother.

Since I became an adult, people have been asking, "Are you two sisters?" Sometimes for fun, we have told a little white lie, and in our Alabama drawl responded, "Why, yes, yes we are." Once we are alone again, we giggle like schoolgirls. It was my lifelong prayer to look like my mother, so the compliment thrilled me. My mother felt flattered that she looked young enough to be mistaken for my sister.

When I joyfully announced that I was going to make her a grandmother for the first time, she was elated. During the time that my husband, David, and I tried to choose the perfect name, my mother made a foreshadowing statement. "Cynthia, since you are the one doing all of the work on having this baby, I think you should be able to name her Mud if you want to."

As the reality began to sink in for her, she worried about what name my unborn daughter should call her. (I think this was a premature concern, but then, of course, you would have to know my sweet mother to understand the dilemma she now faced.)

"I don't want any of those fuddy-duddy, tired old grandmother names like Mimaw or Nana," she told me. "I would like for Elisabeth to call me Honey." In reading back through my journals, I smile now, because I referred to her as Honey for the first eighteen months of my daughter's life. It seemed the perfect name to me, denoting sweetness and, of course, matching the color of my mother's hair.

Like most children, though, Elisabeth had a mind of her own. Living in different states, I only saw my mother every three months. As soon as my daughter could talk, all bets were off on controlling her grandmother's name. When she would visit, Elisabeth would ask me, "Who is that, Mommy?" My response was always, "She is my mother." So Elisabeth walked around the house repeating, "My mudder, my mudder." Thus, Honey turned into Mudder.

After Elisabeth could speak more clearly, she changed the name to Mother. My son, Christian, quickly latched onto the name. When we are all together, people look quizzically at us when they hear my children call her Mother. Explanations are always required at school when my children announce that their "Mother" is coming for a visit.

Only once has the child-given name created a real problem. Around the age of two, Elisabeth and I were leaving Birmingham after a family visit. As I carried her toward the plane, she began thrashing in my arms and screaming, "I want my mother! I want my mother!"

All eyes turned suspiciously on me as if I were kidnapping this child. As I boarded the plane, I kept explaining, "This is really my daughter, she just calls her grandmother 'Mother.'" Sliding into my seat as quickly as possible, I pulled out a bag of M&Ms and began stuffing her full of her first chocolate.

Thank goodness the chocolate calmed her down in the same way it does me. I relaxed and breathed a sigh of relief that no one had called the authorities.

Fast-forward ten years, to my third child, Mary Camille, who decided to change her grandmother's name once more. I am amazed to see how the endearing love of a grandchild can melt the heart of any unsuspecting grandmother. Unable to say Mother, she began by calling her Muddy. My mother thinks that is just the cutest name in the whole world. Now who could have guessed that my sometimes "reserved" mother would ever joyfully embrace the name Mud?

Since that name change, I have realized how love can change any heart. We may start out with preconceived notions of how we will plan and control our own lives, but when unconditional love arrives, our hearts melt. We don't always see it coming, but one day the warmth of that gracious love changes us. And our hearts grow soft in response to his consistent, unwavering, dependable love.

This is love: not that we loved God, but that he loved us and sent his Son as an atoning sacrifice for our sins.
1 John 4:10

'tis the season

Gracie Malone

A man is at his finest
towards the finish of the year;
He is almost what he should be
when the Christmas season's here;
He is less a selfish creature
than at any other time;
When the Christmas spirit rules him
he comes close to the sublime.

Edgar A. Guest

One Christmas Eve, the family gathered in our living room for the reading of a few traditional stories. I selected "The Night Before Christmas," and Joe read the story of Jesus' birth from the New Testament. Afterward we hung our stockings on the mantel and the kids put out cookies and milk for Santa. Then their regular nighttime ritual began. When the first round of potty breaks and drinks of water was winding down, just as I thought the kids were "nestled all snug in their beds," Luke, four, remembered one more thing he wanted to do.

He padded down the hall, ran to the refrigerator, selected a juicy red apple from the crisper, and headed for the front door. As the door creaked on its hinges, he explained, "This is for Santa's reindeer." He carefully placed the fruit on the welcome mat on our front porch.

The next morning, in the excitement of opening gifts and rummaging through stockings stuffed to overflowing with goodies, the special treat for Santa's reindeer was forgotten. Then suddenly Luke remembered. He jumped up, leaping over crumpled paper and ribbons as he made his way to the front door. He dashed outside, then came bursting back in clutching a brownish, wrinkled apple core in his little fist. "Come here!" he shouted. "Everybody come! Hurry!"

We stood in unison and pushed through the front door and went out onto the porch wondering what in the world we would see. Luke was beside himself as he pointed toward the yard. "Look! Those are sled tracks in the grass!"

Sure enough, something very sled-like had cut deep ruts in our lawn. Several of the decorative lightbulbs that lined both sides of our sidewalk were crushed on the cement. It was a convincing scene. Obviously Santa Claus had landed and lifted off right there in our front yard.

Grown-ups as well as all the grandchildren stood wide-eyed. Joe glanced in my direction, shrugged his shoulders, and turned his palms up. The kids jumped up and down in their footed pajamas. After a few minutes, the little ones and their parents made their way back inside. It was then that Joe and I noticed our neighbor who lived three houses away.

He was stumbling around in his pajamas and slippers, rearranging a wooden nativity scene that graced his well-manicured lawn. When he saw us looking in his direction, he yelled, "Looks like somebody got a go-cart for Christmas." Then he repositioned Mary and Joseph in front of the manger, adjusted the make-believe baby in the hay, and picked up a stray lamb. All the while he was straightening things up, he was grumbling loudly, "Ran right through my nativity! I wish they'd stay out of my yard. Those kids are driving me crazy!"

As I watched my neighbor fuss and fume, I couldn't help but think that, like the infamous Scrooge, he needed a good old-fashioned dose of Christmas spirit. The kind of spirit that sees the wonder and joy of the season instead of all the things that are out of sorts. Seems to me, he needed to see Christmas through the eyes of a child.

Shout with joy to God, all the earth! Sing the glory of his name; make his praise glorious!
Psalm 66:1

driver's education 101

Judy Hampton

*Sometimes the heart sees
what is invisible to the eye!*

H. Jackson Brown Jr.

We'd just finished an incredible Thanksgiving meal, and we needed some time to work up an appetite for dessert. I asked my fourteen-year-old grandson if he'd like to go with me in the car.

"Sure, where are we going, Grandma?"

"Oh, you'll see," I said with a grin as we got in my car.

"Grandma, where are we going?" he asked again.

"Well, it's such a beautiful day, I thought it would be a mighty fine time for you to learn how to drive a car."

He shot me a look of wide-eyed glee as his jaw dropped. "Are you serious, Grandma? Does my mom know?"

"Yep, I asked her permission before we left."

His enthusiasm was obvious and his questions continued. "Where are we going? Is it far?"

"I thought we'd go down to the church parking lot. It's probably empty today."

We chattered on as we drove the seemingly endless three miles to the church. Sure enough, the lot was as empty as our hearts were full. "Are you ready?" I asked, knowing that was a silly question. He had been ready to drive since he first stepped into his red and yellow "Little Tikes" toy car that had to be pushed with his feet.

I gave him a few basic instructions: "Don't kill us, and have a good time!" He laughed and got into the driver's seat.

"Buckle up," I said.

He was trembling. "Oh, Grandma, I am so excited. Look at my hands, I'm shaking!"

I continued with clear instructions. "It's so easy, Brandon. Just put your foot on the brake, put the car in gear, and then take your foot off the brake, and push on the gas pedal slowly."

He started off like a pro. Round and round we drove in the huge parking lot. I'd say we went around at least ten jillion times! Then he started weaving in and out of the light poles until I was dizzy.

"Be careful now." I laughed, wondering if the neighbors could see a white car weaving all over an empty parking lot. "Would you like to see if you can park?" I asked.

"No big deal, Grandma."

He pulled right between the white lines as I clapped and exclaimed, "Perfect job! Okay, now back out." Suddenly the car lurched forward onto the curb.

"Stop! Stop! You have it in drive!" I squealed. The tires screeched as he slammed on the brakes. We looked at each other and broke into uncontrollable laughter. It would not have been so funny had he driven through the doors of the church.

He got out to see if he'd burned some rubber. Sure enough, he had. "Well, I guess I should have put it in reverse."

"Hey, it works for me!" I said as my heart left my throat. "What's that out in front of us on the ground up ahead?"

"I don't know, Grandma, I'll stop and see." Brandon put the car in park and walked over to an object lying on the ground. It turned out to be a silver and black leather bracelet, a cheap copy of a well-known brand. He brought it back and gave it to me.

"Grandma, here, I want you to have this bracelet. It's a present from me to you. It is my gift for taking me driving. I am having such a great time."

Accepting his gift, I said, "Thank you so much, sweetheart."

After an hour or so of driving, he asked if he could use my cell phone. "Hello, Mom, guess where I am. I am driving down the 57 freeway going ninety miles an hour in Grandma's car! Hope ya don't mind! We're heading to San Diego." I could hear her laughing. "Let me talk to Grandpa! . . . Grandpa, I was driving Grandma's car down the freeway and hit a truck. Sure hope you don't mind." He giggled.

After the calls, he turned to me. "Grandma, this has been the greatest Thanksgiving Day of my life. Thank you. I will never forget this day."

That did it — he's in the will. Oh, how I love this boy!

Finally it was time to go home and have our dessert. When we reached his street, I asked, "Wanna drive the rest of the way home?"

"Yes-s-s-s-s!" he hissed. He jumped behind the wheel and drove up the street. He gingerly parked in front of his house and then leaned on the horn until all the family came out to cheer.

"Life doesn't get much better than this," I whispered as I got out of the car with a smile on my face. I knew that someday my grandson would be driving his own car. Someday a darling girl would probably be sitting next to him. Someday he might even give her a diamond ring. But today, well, today was a very special day indeed. I had had a date with my grandson — and had a silver bracelet to prove it!

A cheerful heart brings a smile to your face.
Proverbs 15:13 MSG

sweet tarts

Gracie Malone

Pretty much all the honest truth telling in the world is done by children.

Oliver Wendell Holmes Jr.

A few weeks after our son got married, my four-year-old-grandson, Montana, and I were flipping through the album that contained the wedding photos. Of course he was most interested in the pictures of his cousins — six children that would make up our son's blended family. He identified every one of them — Luke, Connor, Mary Catherine, Abby, Ingrid, and Lexi. After naming the children and commenting on their dressy clothes, he pointed to the main characters in the drama.

"There's Uncle Matt and that's Aunt Rachel and . . ."

He turned his face toward mine and with furrowed brow asked, "Grandma Gracie, who is that guy?" He was pointing to the rather dignified gentleman in the center of the picture.

"Oh, that man is the minister," I answered.

"The mister?" Montana seemed confused.

"No, honey, the minister — you know, the preacher."

"Oh." The little guy seemed to understand as he turned the page.

Then he began naming the people in the next shot. "There's Uncle Matt, that's Aunt Rachel, and there's the Creature."

Later I found myself chuckling about what Montana had said and wondered if that's the worst thing that minister had been called. Irreverent though it may seem, I must admit the guy with his gray-cropped beard and unusual pointed hairline did have an out-of-this-world appearance. I couldn't hold back a wicked giggle.

Shortly afterward, I had an interesting conversation with Montana's big brother, Myles, five. Seems he had developed a less-than-creature-like relationship with the leadership at his church — Fellowship of the Woodlands. In fact, Myles never wants to miss a single event. I can't say I blame him when I think about the kid-friendly

81

meetings that take place on that campus. For one thing they have a train made of brightly colored barrels that Myles and his mom take a ride in almost every time they pull in the parking lot.

Myles' fervor for toddler-style worship became evident one evening when our son Mike and daughter-in-law Jeanna were feeling a bit ambivalent about going to church. After lounging around the house most of Saturday afternoon, they just couldn't seem to get motivated to get dressed and go. Myles would hear nothing of it. He overheard their should-we, should-we-not conversation and made the decision for them.

"Well," he declared, "I'm going! You guys better get ready." He ran to his room and started changing clothes. What could Mike and Jeanna do but pull on some clean clothes and run to the car? When Jeanna told me this story later, I felt the buttons popping on my blouse. My "strong-willed" little grandson had made a "strong" decision in the right direction and proved a truth that Jesus taught his disciples centuries ago. There are many times in our lives when "a little child shall lead them."

I thank you, Father, Master of heaven

and earth, that you hid these things from the know-it-alls and showed them to these innocent newcomers. Yes, Father, it pleased you to do it this way.

Luke 10:21 MSG

grandma's matchmaking service

Bonnie Afman Emmorey

Two of my grandsons were playing marbles when a pretty little girl walked by. "I'll tell you," said Jake to J.D., "when I stop hating girls, that's the one I'm going to stop hating first."

Encyclopedia of Humor

Coming from a family of true romantics, I shouldn't have been surprised — but I was. My oldest son, Nathan, a college student, wanted me to be his matchmaker. In fact, when I would return home from ministry trips, he would phone to ask if I had met any interesting young women he should meet. I set him up with intriguing and fun email correspondence with lovely candidates from across the country, which included a beauty queen, a professional singer, a chalk artist, and several dynamic and captivating university students. Many friendships developed, and I felt that any one of these women would have fit very nicely into our family, but somehow nothing more came of my "setups."

My sons' godly grandma, my own mother, has been praying for both my sons' future wives since before they were born. In fact, Mother calls me often, inquiring about their current love interests. So when Nathan called Grandma and asked her also to be "the matchmaker," I don't think she was surprised at all.

Nate had noticed some very attractive and fascinating young women at Grandma and Grandpa's church and decided that Grandma was the perfect go-between. Knowing she is a wonderful cook and that hospitality is her gift, he asked her to check on the availability of the potential blind dates and to feel free to set up a dinner engagement for him.

My mother was born for a job like this. She did the research and made the calls. She found an appropriate prospect and set up the date. She cooked a delicious meal and everything was perfect — including dessert. Of course, I had to call when a few hours had passed and I hadn't heard a thing. The suspense was killing me! Mother answered the phone and let me know that everything was fine. "The kids" were taking a stroll down their picturesque country road after dinner. She said the conversation at the dinner table had flowed easily, and she was quite pleased with her matchmaking. She was sure Nate would call me later. He did just that and told me he had a very enjoyable evening.

My mind went back to earlier years. Nathan had grown up hearing stories of Grandma and Grandpa's romantic love story. It was considerably better than most books or movies. Both of my parents were engaged to someone else when they met, but that didn't stop Grandpa from knowing a good thing when he saw it. It wasn't long before they both knew they were meant for each other, and then the excitement really started. They eloped — and kept their marriage a secret for a full month. Grandma's dramatic love story is one of Nate's favorites. In fact, he has been known to use it for the entertainment portion of his own dates. You may have already guessed he has also inherited his grandmother's storytelling abilities.

That blind date was neither the first nor the last of Nathan's dates at Grandma's house. He loves her cooking, her prayers, and her tolerance of his teasing, but he especially appreciates her interest in match-making. So far the effort has not produced a permanent result — but it has challenged her to continue to pray that her grandsons find Christian spouses who will pass on a legacy of faith to future generations.

She is clothed with strength and dignity; she can laugh at the days to come. She speaks with wisdom, and faithful instruction is on her tongue.
Proverbs 31:25–26

"wanna play, grandma?"

Gracie Malone

*Part of being a champ
is acting like a champ.
You have to learn how to win
and not run away when you lose.*

Nancy Kerrigan

For most of us grandmas there's nothing more enjoyable than playing with our grandkids, especially when we realize we're helping them grow socially and develop important skills. I've noticed how playing games has helped our little ones learn to listen and observe as well as to follow directions and solve problems. Some games teach important concepts, like sportsmanship, and others provide valuable information.

Montana, our five-year-old, loves to play with his Name the Animal cards. We've been "naming the animals" since he was old enough to talk. The cards portray sixty-five different creatures identified in big block letters. On the back, there's information about the animal's characteristics and way of life. When I flash a card, Montana yells out the proper name. Sometimes we talk about the facts on the back of the card, but identifying the creature is counted a win. As Montana stacks up the cards he can identify, I "win" the ones he can't. Yeah, I know the cards are stacked against me. There's a sucker born every minute and in my house — for the sake of the kids — I keep being reborn.

Through the years, Montana has learned a lot about animals, and the cards have even helped him learn to read as he tries to sound out some of the names beneath the picture. Besides that, as we've interacted with each other, I've had the sheer fun of seeing his sense of humor bloom like pansies opening to the morning sun. One day I was flabbergasted when he couldn't identify the aardvark, and then he called the zebra a giraffe and the rhino an elephant. After he saw I was genuinely confused, he giggled and said, "I tricked you, Grandma Gracie! You thought I didn't know them!"

Not all the games we play provide usable data. Some are just-for-fun games that actually have very little redeeming value; others border on the ridiculous. In the latter category is another of Montana's favorites — a classic card game called "Old Maid."

It's a simple game where each person tries to collect the most pairs by choosing randomly from your opponent's concealed hand. As you match pairs, you just can't help but identify with the funny characters. I love being Bertha the Ballerina, and Montana's favorite is Freddie the Fireman. But neither of us likes to get the Old Maid card.

If you end up with her, you're declared the "Old Maid," and you lose the game. Montana hoots and hollers when I draw the dreaded card. I think it's because she looks so, well, grandmotherly. She has a tight knot of gray hair pinned up with two knitting needles, and her wrinkled face is painted with circles of pink blush and a trace of red lipstick. Dressed in an old gray sweater with an afghan covering her lap, she sits slumped in her rocking chair.

"That's you!" Montana giggles as I plop the card face up on the table.

"That woman is definitely not me," I say.

Montana knows full well I'm not the rocking chair type. In fact, I take great pride in being off my rocker and into mischief and fun. Nevertheless, a verbal tug-of-war takes place until one of us gives up and deals the cards again. Every time my grandkids and I get together, some game-playing madness takes place.

Recently Mike, Jeanna, Montana, and Myles arrived for an overnight visit. I heard the back door open and glanced up as Montana rounded the corner into the living room where I was sitting on the sofa. When he realized I was talking on the phone, he stopped dead in his tracks and waited for me to push the off button. I couldn't wait to give my precious grandboy a big hug.

As I wrapped my arms around him, his very first words were, "What do you wanna play?"

I couldn't hold back a giggle as I turned my palms up and said, "Whatever!" Then I quickly added, "You pick the game, I'll get the cookies and milk."

I do not consider myself yet to have taken hold of it. But one thing I do: Forgetting what is behind and straining toward what is ahead, I press on toward the goal to win the prize.
Philippians 3:13–14

come unto me, all you who are ornery

Lynn Warren

Have you ever noticed that grandchildren do not carry pictures of their grandparents?

Charlie Jarvis

For the first half century of her life, Grandma Maggie was what some would call a character. Let's just say there wasn't a skeleton in her closet — there was a whole boneyard!

But when Grandpa Joe got religion, Grandma wasn't far behind. They shucked off their old lives and latched "whole hog" onto their new faith. Most of their eight children and nearly a hundred grand-, great-, and great-great-grandchildren found the change downright aggravating.

For Pete's sake! They even got rid of their TV! There wasn't anything to do at their house when you went to visit except talk

Scripture. That got old fast. As one of the few Christians in the clan, even I got winded in conversations with Grandpa. But you had to admire him and Grandma. God really had changed their lives, and they were determined to rescue every sinner they met in their remaining years.

Right in line with the national averages, Grandpa got sick first. Joe and Maggie had given up their Marlboros when they met Jesus, but lung cancer paid no mind to that. They'd lit up for fifty years, and now it was time to pay the piper.

Lung cancer is a dirty disease that doesn't take you down easy. But Grandpa surprised us all by holding tightly to his Lord all the way to the end.

I remember our last time together — me kneeling beside Grandpa as he lay on the couch, holding his hand as he wheezed into an oxygen mask. But his eyes were still bright, and he promised to meet me in heaven someday. Somehow, I knew he would.

Seven years later, I knelt beside the same couch holding Grandma Maggie's hand as she labored against the same foe. The fight was no cleaner this time; she couldn't even raise her bald head off the pillow. Grandma never had a high threshold for pain. In fact

— and I mean no disrespect — Maggie was a natural hypochondriac. She always had an irritating tendency to whine at the slightest ache. Even loving her as we did, the family cringed when cancer was diagnosed.

But in her suffering, Grandma surprised us just as Grandpa had.

I overheard my mama and the Hospice worker commenting on how Grandma never complained. Maggie took on a sweetness in the face of death, knowing her future was secure in Christ.

On our last visit, I leaned close and listened as Maggie whispered her love for Jesus. Her eyes pierced me as she spoke of her oldest boy, my father. He had cried at her bedside a few nights earlier, his head bent in unaccustomed prayer for his mama. My heart jumped at her words about my father: "Your papa can be a holy terror, but I've never given up hope that someday he will be saved."

Grandma continued, "Your daddy asked me what I wanted for Christmas. I told him I wanted a cross." Her eyes twinkled. "Go take a look at it."

As I gazed at the delicate gold crucifix stretched out on her nightstand, I knew the cross was for Papa, not for her.

"He loves you so much, Grandma. He's

just frustrated with not being able to fight this, and it's tearing him up. If he would only let go, and let God help him . . ."

"I know, honey," Grandma Maggie whispered. "I pray for him constantly." Our eyes met, and in that moment we bonded as never before.

Grandma wasn't the one dying; my daddy was. Spiritually. My grandmother and I stood on either side, the generation before and the generation after, petitioning God for my father's soul.

Then she tired and I kissed her good-bye.

Our family is filled with late bloomers when it comes to God. We tend to be a stubborn bunch, and it's a good thing for us the Spirit is so doggone persistent.

I was a relative pup, only fifteen years old, when the lightning struck. My little girl began her walk of faith when she was only five. I'm thankful that my daughter has an extra ten years to walk with the Lord I didn't experience. I wish we could be "born saved" and not waste any time at all.

Papa is retiring this spring — without God and without his mother. My mama has always followed in his wake, going where he goes, lodging where he lodges, and dodging what he dodges. But when he turns his heart around, I bet she will too.

The good Lord is patient and unwilling to lose anybody, including my hardheaded daddy. When the time is right, Papa will slip that yoke on and admire its perfect fit. And Grandma will smile in heaven, waiting to welcome her boy home.

Come to me, all you who are weary and burdened, and I will give you rest. Take my yoke upon you and learn from me.
Matthew 11:28–29

words: the good, the bad, and the funny

Gracie Malone

*I know why families were created
with all their imperfections.
They humanize you.*

Anaïs Nin

One night my daughter-in-law Jeanna confided, "Gracie, I felt so bad about something that happened this morning. I heard a loud crash coming from the bathroom, followed by a blood-curdling scream. I just knew Montana had broken an arm or cut himself. I ran as fast as I could from the kitchen to the bathroom. I didn't know what I'd see when I rounded that corner."

"Oh, my goodness! What happened?"

"Well" — Jeanna took a deep breath — "when I got there, Montana was draped across the side of the bathtub, the shower curtain was crumpled around him, and he was clutching a piece of broken plastic. You

97

know that gadget that holds our shampoo and soap? Seems he had been swinging on it like it was jungle gym. When it broke, he fell and landed on his back, right on the side of the tub. Anyway, other than a bad bruise he seems to be okay. But we were both so scared!"

"Well, honey, accidents like that happen — especially with little boys like ours. Why do you feel bad about it? You know, mothers can't be everywhere."

"I know. It's just that, well . . . I didn't respond the way I wish I had." She paused. "Oh, Gracie, when I burst through that door and realized he was okay, I yelled so loud he stopped the crying and his eyes bugged out. Besides that, I said a bad word."

"It's okay." I patted her on the leg sympathetically.

I wanted to tell her that Montana wouldn't remember what she'd said, but, alas, I'd already heard the story from the perspective of a five-year-old.

"Grandma Gracie," Montana had whispered, "my mom said a bad word."

"Well, I'm sure she's sorry about that. You know, son, sometimes grown-ups make mistakes just like kids do. I know she feels bad about it. You need to forgive your mother."

"Yeah." He shrugged, paused, and then added something that made my eyes bug out. "Grandma Gracie, she said the 'F' word."

I felt my blood pressure rising as I thought, this kid's way too young to know such a word exists. But I had yet to hear the whole story.

"Grandma Gracie, do you know what the 'F' word is?" Montana asked.

"I think I do." I swallowed hard and asked, "Do you?"

"Yep!" He picked at a string on his jeans for several minutes. "I'll tell you what the 'F' word is if you promise not to go Aghhhhhhhhh!" (I couldn't help but grin as I thought, this kid knows his grandma so well!)

Now, I ask you, all you grandmas, what would you have done?

I promised. "Tell me, Montana, what is the 'F' word?" I braced myself.

Montana wiped his forehead and exhaled loudly. I could tell this kid really hated to tell on his mom. After a long pause, he cupped his hand around his mouth and, in a subdued tone, spat out the word "butt."

I jumped up and ran out of the room. I needed a place where I could giggle and gather my wits about me. I should have remembered Montana was too young to spell. Why, he barely knew the alphabet! But somewhere he'd heard the phrase "F word" and I guess he figured all bad words fit into the "F" category.

I decided it was time to tell his mother what Montana had said. Besides that, it was too good a story to keep to myself. As we sat huddled on the sofa in front of the fire, we both laughed shamelessly, then launched into a long discussion about reactions and how to handle them.

"It's not easy to control what we say," I said, "especially when it comes to a knee-jerk reaction. I've mumbled a few 'bad words' myself at times."

"Well," Jeanna said, "if you didn't goof up now and then, I wouldn't love you so much." Then she said with a grin, "I think it's time I get off my rear end and go to bed."

We get it wrong nearly every time we open our mouths. If you could find someone whose speech was perfectly true, you'd have a perfect person, in perfect control of life.
James 3:2 MSG

no peas, please!

Jennie Afman Dimkoff

Waste not, want not!

Benjamin Franklin

The spoon loomed closer. At eye level now, it swam before my eyes. My stomach roiled as the smell of canned green peas assailed me. Bile rose in the back of my throat. Just as the grip of steely fingers fastened themselves around my chin, I woke with a start!

Relief flooded over me. It had been a dream. As I lay back and drew a tremulous breath, the reality of what had prompted the nightmare came to me. She was coming tomorrow. Grandma Gertrude was coming for a whole week — and she always brought canned peas.

"Jennie Beth, wake up, honey! You'll be late for the bus. You have to eat your breakfast and get into your Halloween costume!" Mother's voice was too cheerful after a night filled with pea green dreams, but I groggily dragged myself downstairs and then got caught up in the excitement of the day. Mother brushed my long hair and fitted a wide white band with a hand-stitched red cross attached to the front. "You are going to be the prettiest seven-year-old nurse at the party," Mother assured me with a kiss. Her huge stomach stood between us, and I rested my cheek against it for a moment.

"Will our baby come today, Mama?" I asked.

"I think maybe it will," she responded. "Hurry now, or you and Carol will be late."

"Does Grandma have to come, Mama? I don't want her here!"

"Jennie! Don't say such a thing! Grandma is going to help us while I go to the hospital. You be a good girl and help with your little sisters. And make sure you eat everything Grandma puts on your plate. You know how much that means to her."

Swallowing back a fresh wave of nausea, I left for school, wishing that I could be a real nurse and go to the hospital with mother instead.

At recess, I told my friend Clara that Grandma was coming. Her response amazed me. "You're so lucky," she said with envy. "I wish my grandma could come today. Nana brings treats in her purse and reads me stories."

Her comments left me more depressed. We didn't have a nice name like Nana to call our grandma. In fact, I secretly referred to her as Grandma No No because she never let us do anything fun — and the only treat she ever brought was canned peas.

On the ride home from school a familiar car passed the bus with the driver honking and waving. Stopping at the next corner, our father got out and waved for the bus to stop. I'd never seen Daddy so excited. "It's a *boy!*" he shouted, "a *boy!*" Carol and I were allowed to leave the bus and ride the rest of the way home with our jubilant parent who, after fathering four daughters, had been given a son that day.

Grandma Gertrude actually smiled when Daddy excitedly told her the news — especially after hearing that the little boy would be called Ben after her late husband and Daddy's father.

"There will finally be an Afman to carry on the family name," she said with a hint of approval and then abruptly tackled dinner preparations. I eyed the can of peas staring at me from the kitchen counter. It was standing on end, at exactly my height, and I knew that Grandma No No and I would be at the table for an hour longer than any of the others once again, locked in a battle of wills until my plate was empty.

That night when Daddy got home from the hospital, we talked.

"Daddy, how come Grandma Gertrude is so mean?"

"Well, I don't believe she thinks she's being mean at all."

"But she force feeds me things I hate. She won't let me leave the table until the last bite is gone, and she won't let me do anything I want to do."

"Well, did you know that your Grandpa Ben died when I was only sixteen years old?" Daddy sighed. "To be honest, your grandpa had a drinking problem, Jennie, and he didn't provide for his wife and four children very well. Sometimes Grandma's canned peas were all we had for supper. Her life has been hard, but she raised me and your aunts and uncle all by herself. Will you try to be thankful for Grandma this week?"

The next day I took a new look at Grandma Gertrude. Her severe black dress was still the same and her stockings continued to flatten long threads of hair against her unshaven legs, but I noticed something else too. She never wasted anything and every action she took was for a purpose.

Many years have passed since that memorable week. Grandma Gertrude is in heaven now, along with both her daughters. I like to think of her there — loving God and learning to smile and to rest in his care. I learned some important lessons from her, like vegetables are good for you, work hard, avoid waste, and don't give up when life is difficult — and someday, when I'm a grandmother myself, to never, never, never visit my grandchildren bearing canned peas. And I hope she would be pleased that today I am a published author with the name Afman in my title.

Listen to your father, who gave you life,
and do not despise your [grand] mother
when she is old.
Proverbs 23:22

betwixt
tweens and teens

Gracie Malone

Hire a teen
while he still knows everything.

Bumper sticker

I've got one thing to say about grandparenting teens. It's a lot more fun than parenting them. While their moms and dads are dealing with our grandkids' "coming of age" and handling all sorts of complicated issues like curfews, cars, and companions, we grandmas are free to simply watch them grow — physically, spiritually, emotionally.

Observing our two oldest grandsons develop from precocious kids into a presumptuous teen and a fun-loving "tween" has not only been enjoyable, it's been stimulating and more than a little refreshing. For example, I called one day to see if Luke (now a strapping fourteen-year-old) and his younger brother Connor (twelve) could mow our lawn. Luke listened politely while I described the task at hand, including mowing and edging the sidewalk. I thought Connor could use the leaf blower, "whack" the weeds along the fence, and sweep the deck in our backyard. I finished my sales pitch with, "Since your job as soccer referee is now over, I thought you could make a little money to sock away for a rainy day."

Luke cleared his throat and in a business-like tone replied, "Well, thanks for asking us to work for you. I'll talk to my people and get back to you in the morning."

I couldn't help but laugh as I hung up the phone. I imagined Luke, mercenary individual that he is, rubbing his palms together before sliding down the banister to the living room and landing smack in the middle of his "people" to discuss the new job opportunity.

A few days later, after Luke's people had given permission, he and Connor showed up for work. They did a super job taking care of our lawn for a modest twenty bucks and provided entertainment completely free of charge.

As Joe helped Connor manage the complicated task of "weed-whacking," I asked him about school. "Connor, I know it feels good for school to be out for the summer. By the way, how were your grades?"

"Great!" Connor quipped in his usual staccato manner. "I made A and B's."

Of course he was hoping I wouldn't notice the missing plural ending on the A. I laughed as I thought, *Ahhh, sweet freedom!* My grandma status leaves me completely free to enjoy Connor's cute personality and let his mom and dad decide whether or not "A and B's" are good enough.

When the lawn-mowing project was completed, the four of us relaxed in our living room sipping from bottles of Arizona Stress Tea and chatting about one of Luke's favorite topics — the current movies. "Papa Joe, we need to go see the new 'X-Men' film. You want to go with us, Grandma Gracie?"

"No, Luke, as you know, I really don't enjoy action films." I shifted on the sofa and continued knowingly, "In fact, I just can't get into those creatures that morph from one thing to another. Give me a good old-fashioned dose of reality, a film with a story line and a touch of romance, and I'll be there!"

"Grandma Gracie," Luke muttered, "you need to try something different, you know, vary your viewing experiences, expand your repertoire. And, it seems to me you don't know much about X-Men." He twisted his lips into a playful grin and added, "For one thing, they don't 'morph.' They are mutants." He shrugged his shoulders and turned his palms up as he added, "Mutants don't morph!"

"Mutants don't morph?" At that, all four of us burst out laughing at the absurdity of our conversation.

After Luke and Connor went home, I recorded the newly discovered tidbit of information in my notebook so I wouldn't forget it. I now offer it to grandmothers everywhere — free of charge. For one never knows when such info might come in handy.

As your grandchildren morph (or mutate) from preadolescent tween into a full-fledged, key-carrying teen, there may be times when their choices are troublesome, their antics less than funny. Still, they need "people" who believe in them wholeheartedly and love them unconditionally. And, perhaps most importantly, they need people who will simply listen and laugh at their stories.

*One generation will
commend your works to another;
they will tell of your mighty acts.*
Psalm 145:4

brown sugar sandwiches

Vicki Tiede

One hundred years from now . . . it will not matter what your bank account was, the sort of house you lived in, or the kind of car you drove . . . but the world may be different because you were important in the life of a child.

Found on a wall plaque

In 1949, when I was only two years old, twins were born into our family. My biological grandparents had passed away, so while my mother was in the hospital, I stayed with the elderly couple across the road. I knew them as Grandpa Art and Art's Mama.

Art's Mama was really his wife, but as a toddler I didn't understand the nuances of relationships and their titles. Art's Mama always wore a smile and a cotton dress with a full apron. She was kind and attentive and protected me from their scary pet boxer in a no-nonsense tone of voice. Everything I know about being a grandma to my six grandchildren I learned from Grandpa Art and Art's Mama.

When Mother went into labor, Dad walked me across the road to Grandpa Art and Art's Mama's farm. When Grandpa Art saw me coming down the long driveway he called out, "Here comes My Sally!" That's what my "adopted" grandparents always called me — My Sally. That pet name was an assurance I was loved and cherished.

My mother had to stay in the hospital for a week after the birth of my twin sisters. I had never been away from her before. Grandpa Art and Art's Mama knew this might be scary for me, and they made every effort to make my visit comfortable.

That week I had a terrible cold. Art's Mama concocted a home remedy made with smelly goose grease, and Grandpa Art attempted to put it on my neck and wrap it with an old gray sock. I flat-out refused to put that ugly old thing around my neck. Grandpa Art bent down, looked into my eyes, and assured me, "It will make your cold go away." As they fastened that old wool sock around my neck, Grandpa encouraged me in his gravelly, German-accented voice that I loved, "That's My

111

Sally." I wore that sock for two entire days and refused to let them take it off.

Art's Mama made a special bed for me on the couch while I stayed with them. In their old farmhouse, they slept upstairs — but not that week. Grandpa Art insisted, "I can't possibly leave My Sally alone." Art's Mama made a bed on the floor beside the couch and that's where they slept, never leaving my side. The next morning I woke up in an unfamiliar place, but before long, Art's Mama pulled me up to the kitchen table and poured me a cup of coffee.

"We are gonna make this taste real good now," Grandpa Art promised as he loaded it with milk and sugar. For me the fun was more about stirring this sweet treat, licking the spoon when I finished, and spending time with Grandpa Art and Art's Mama than actually drinking the coffee. Grandpa Art insisted, "No cuppa coffee's complete without open-faced brown sugar sandwiches." With that declaration, my grandparents taught me how to use the back of my teaspoon to pat the crunchy brown sugar onto a slice of buttered bread "just so" in order to prevent the sugar from falling off before it reached my mouth. This became our daily routine. Art's Mama smiled and made me feel like I was the most special guest she'd ever had.

Grandpa Art always wore bib overalls, and in the skinny front pocket he always carried an Almond Joy candy bar — and I knew there were two small candy bars in that package. He'd tell me, "The best part about an Almond Joy is that there are always two — one for me and one for My Sally." Art's Mama would smile, and I noticed she took great delight in the fun I had with Grandpa Art.

During that special week of my two-year-old life, I was given a gift that would become my model for being a grandma. Communicating unconditional love and commitment to my grandchildren comes naturally as I call them by special pet names and when I get down on their level to look them in the eyes. When we share a "cuppa coffee" together, our hearts are filled to the brim. I have, however, discovered that too many brown sugar sandwiches mixed with caffeine isn't always the best diet — so we save that treat for special occasions.

One thing we agree on is that nothing is sweeter than sharing something treasured with someone you love. Most importantly, I learned that the greatest gift of all is to give your time and love to your grandchildren, as I pass on the legacy of Art's Mama to those I love.

My children, love must not be
a matter of words or talk;
It must be genuine,
and show itself in action.
1 John 3:18 NEB

ho, ho holidays

Gracie Malone

Then the Grinch thought of something he hadn't before! "Maybe Christmas," he thought, "doesn't come from a store. Maybe Christmas . . . perhaps . . . means a little bit more."

Dr. Seuss,
How the Grinch Stole Christmas

I'd pictured a Norman Rockwell Christmas — one with the family decked out in red velvet dresses and crisp white shirts dining on glazed carved ham and steaming scalloped potatoes, Christmas tree lights sparkling in the background.

But that day — Christmas, of all days — the water main broke.

Our oldest son, Matt, had no sooner arrived with his four kids than our son Mike's four-year-old Myles popped through our back door and announced, "Dere's waddah

115

gushing from the middah of de dwiveway!" He jumped up and down excitedly and added, "Lots of it — a big waddahfall wunning down the stweet. Come look evahbody!"

With that pronouncement, we all pushed through the door to see what was up. Sure enough, Myles had described the scene well. We had to find a way to stop the flow. Luke and twelve-year-old Connor climbed through the bushes in front looking for the shutoff while the older members of the family tried to find the key for the water meter box. We looked like a bunch of adrenalin-charged clowns racing around the yard and rummaging through tools in our garage. It took at least thirty minutes to get the "waddah" turned off, leaving us drenched and dirty.

Instead of red velvet dresses and crisp white shirts, we had men with mud on their blue jeans and kids with dirt and grass stuck to their tennis shoes, standing in a circle in the Malones' kitchen. The Christmas ham and cheesy potatoes were cooling on the stove. And the vegetables, well, they were still in the freezer. My daughter-in-law Jeanna and I shot stricken glances at each other as reality sunk in. We had no running water — nary a drip from the faucets, not a drop to even make tea. As I turned toward the gang that included three sons, six grandkids, and one frazzled husband, I didn't know what else to do but turn my palms up, shrug my shoulders and grin. "Well, folks, have some ham!"

Without a moment's hesitation grandson Luke took the carving knife in hand and began passing slices of meat speared on its tip to his dad, brother, and granddad. Before I could locate some paper plates and ask, "Potatoes anyone?" the room was filled with laughter and boisterous details of the crisis that had just unfolded.

Thus, we dined — well actually, we picnicked — most of us standing around the kitchen as we planned how to survive the night. Thankfully, I'd stocked our fridge with "designer" drinking water, and we had two gallons of spring water in the garage for hand-washing. Jeanna and Luke decided they could keep the commodes in usable condition by filling the tanks with water from the swimming pool. (Their idea became a bucket brigade that lasted throughout the night.)

With a workable plan in mind, we gathered around our tree, read the Christmas story from the Bible, opened gifts, devoured a plate of chocolate fudge, and finally settled into an assortment of cots and beds. As I drifted off to sleep I lamented about what our family missed by having to celebrate this significant occasion in such a haphazard way.

I shouldn't have worried. The next day we located a compassionate plumber who mended our water line, and we shared a nice family breakfast. Afterward, I asked each person what they enjoyed most about our unique celebration. Jeanna loved our new nine-foot tree sparkling with a thousand tiny lights. The grandkids loved their new games and toys. The guys grunted, almost in unison, "Ugh, meat! Served on a knife." When the giggles died down, little Myles jumped out of his chair and shouted, "Gamma Gacie, I just wuvved that waddah! Whoooosh! All dat waddah was way cool!"

We all burst out laughing. Later, after my kids and the grandkids had climbed into their cars and departed, I sighed deeply as I recognized something important. Christmas, after all, isn't about glitz, glitter, and perfectionism. It's about love and laughter and the feeling of deep content that comes from simply being together and solving problems as a team. Now I'm wondering what kind of bonding experience I can come up with for next Christmas!

I bring you good news of great joy that will be for all the people. Today in the town of David a Savior has been born to you; he is Christ the Lord.
Luke 2:10–11

the pickle party

Carol Kent

The best thing to spend on children is time.

Anonymous

The invitation was irresistible. An exclusive, five-star hotel chain was launching a new business venture that involved selling time-shares. We received a too-good-to-be-true offer to stay for four nights in a deluxe condominium located in a swanky resort community. They advertised in-room Jacuzzi bathtubs and the property had three pools, a golf course, tennis courts, and fine restaurants. The location was only a forty-five-minute drive from our grandchildren — and if we were willing to sit through a ninety-minute presentation on why we should buy into "this astoundingly reasonable opportunity of a lifetime," we could enjoy all of the amenities for four days at a minuscule price. We set the dates and invited my sister Bonnie to join us, along with our two granddaughters.

Arriving at our "home away from home," we were delighted to discover the facility lived up to the description in the color brochure. Chelsea and Hannah squealed with delight as they tried to decide which of the three large pools they would try first. After swimming to their hearts' content, the girls went to the recreation building and played ping pong, bocce ball, shuffleboard, and basketball. (We were definitely getting our money's worth out of this adventure!)

The next day, my daughter-in-law April took Chelsea shopping. It didn't take eight-year-old Hannah long to investigate the Jacuzzi in the master suite. "Grammy," she exclaimed, "there's a bathtub big enough to be a pool right here in your bedroom! Let's go swimming in here!"

Hannah, Aunt Bonnie, and I donned our swimming suits and filled the tub with water and bubbles. Bonnie (my most frugal and financially disciplined sister) had made a trip to the Dollar Store earlier where she had purchased a jar of dill pickles. We had no other treats, so we piled a plate full of pickles and took them with us to the tub.

Before long, conversation started to get

deep — three women in a tub, leisurely discussing the challenges and complexities of life. I eagerly looked for a window of opportunity for a heart connection with my young Hannah. We decided to call our Jacuzzi outing "The Pickle Party," and we promptly took turns picking dill pickles off the plate as we chatted and munched our way through the next hour.

"Hannah," I said, "what's the best part of today?"

Her response was right on: "Talking to girls about being a woman is *definitely* the best part of today." Her older sister, Chelsea, had recently entered puberty and this was of great fascination to Hannah.

We discussed her conflicts with her sister. "We just don't get along with each other," she stated dispassionately. "I think our personalities are too different, and besides, she's always getting me into trouble." I knew the part about *who* got *whom* into trouble could be debated, but I decided to move to "higher ground" in our conversation.

Aunt Bonnie said she was turning into a prune, so that left me alone with Hannah, where we could move into more intimate conversation. "How do you think I can help you best, Hannah?" I asked.

"Well," she said, admiring her image in the big mirror next to the tub, "I think you can teach me about how to be a good mom. And I'll need to learn how to do laundry and housework." Her mind was moving in many directions. "And if I have kids, I don't think I can have a job too. But you have a job, don't you, Grammy, and your kid is my Daddy." I could see the wheels turning in her brain. Big decisions. Major choices.

"Hannah," I said seriously, "Grammy's been praying for your future husband."

Her eyes grew big and she laughed out loud. "It's too early to pray for my husband, Grammy. I'm just a kid."

I piled her soapy hair on top of her head in a coiffure as I said, "It's never too early to pray about who you're going to marry. It's one of the most important decisions of your lifetime."

"Well, that's not going to happen for a long time," she stated emphatically, "but thanks for praying for me." Then, chomping down her sixth dill pickle, she abruptly added, "And you need to teach me how to handle high electrical bills." With that final comment, she decided we had taken enough time for grown-up discussion, and it was time to dunk our heads in the water and play.

We made a memory that day — Grammy and Hannah — having a pickle party amongst talk of puberty, sibling rivalry, boys, and grown-up matters. And from this day forward, every time we bite into a dill pickle, we'll both remember the closeness we shared that day.

Point your [grand] kids in the right direction — when they're old they won't be lost.
Proverbs 22:6 MSG

it's about time

Gracie Malone

Happiness is as a butterfly, which when pursued is always just beyond your grasp, but which, if you will sit down quietly, may alight upon you.

Nathaniel Hawthorne

When my grandkids are visiting, I look for opportunities to "hang out" with them, even if it's for only a few minutes. It doesn't take much time to put my arm around their shoulders and observe their current model-building project or settle beside them on the sofa to watch an inning of a baseball game or part of a movie. When I make myself available, I often find they open up and talk about things important to them, such as problems they're having with friends or some of the challenges they face in school. This is how intimacy develops. As an added bonus, we hear some of the funniest stories we'll ever hear — tales that get passed down from one generation to the next.

One afternoon I was determined to take a little time out for meaningful interaction with our four-year-old grandson, Connor. I enticed him to sit beside me on the patio by offering him a box of apple juice and a couple of cookies. As he sipped the juice and munched on the sugary snack, I could tell that Connor was lapsing into a pensive mood. (Little Connor is our deep thinker — a child whose personality, at least from his dad's point of view, causes him to view life from a perspective that's "a bit on the dark side.")

The quiet moments on our deck provided a perfect opportunity for Connor and me to share some "deep thoughts." After watching the wheels of his little brain spin silently for a few moments, I asked a question that members of my generation ask young ones all the time: "Connor, have you thought about what you want to be when you grow up?"

He gazed at the clouds, then he turned to me and said, "Grandma Gracie, when I grow up I want to be a horse."

A horse! Not a horseback rider. Not a cowboy. But a horse!

I stifled a giggle, knowing such an irreverent reaction would end our serious conversation. Instead, I cupped my hand under my chin, Freudian style, and reflected back his words. "Hmmm, a horse, huh?"

"Yep! A horse."

There was no word of explanation — just a simple declaration that left me scratching my graying head in utter amazement. Then he jumped down from his chair and ran toward the swing in our big oak tree.

Later that night as I settled in my bed, my mind returned to the conversation with Connor as I wondered what in the world he was thinking. Then I got a visual picture of a sleek black stallion running through flowered meadows — muscles rippling, cool breezes blowing through his mane. I pictured him grazing in lush green pastures, drinking from cool mountain streams. As I drifted off to sleep, I decided Connor had a darn good idea.

There are some days I would gladly trade places with a horse.

He makes me lie down in green pastures, he leads me beside quiet waters, he restores my soul.
Psalm 23:2–3

spin the bottle

Diana Pintar

*If you don't have a little bit of heartache,
how do you know when you're happy?*

Jane Powell

As empty nesters, my husband, Mike, and I
lived a quiet, well-ordered life in our
"barely-big-enough-for-two" detached
condominium. As is true of many life-
changing circumstances, the ring of the telephone signaled the end of one season in our
lives and the beginning of the next.

Barely intelligible through her sobbing,
my daughter, Cori, cried, "Mom? We need
your help!" Her marriage had ended.
Without financial resources, she and her
seven-month-old son, Carson, needed a
place to live.

Mike and I moved over to make room for
the refugees. The entire downstairs of our
home, a walkout that previously accommo-

dated our home office and library, became their new home. We squeezed the former contents of those rooms into our tiny guestroom. We crammed baby food and baby bottles into our already overcrowded kitchen, and we purchased a high chair.

Next, we set some basic ground rules to safeguard our physical and emotional boundaries:

- That chair is Mike's.
- If that door is closed, it means, "Do not enter! Don't even knock!"
- Take off your shoes when walking on the hardwood floors so you don't wake the baby.

Childproofing everything was our final priority. With tears in my eyes, I packed up my "breakables" and "unsafe-ables" and stored them in Styrofoam-filled boxes. We hauled a battle-scarred table from our basement storage to replace our tipsy and therefore hazardous glass-topped coffee table. With adhesive strips, we attached ugly corner protectors to the table to guard against bumps and bruises. Duct tape became a necessary adornment as the tiny strips failed to hold up to inquisitive toddler fingers. With the addition of a playpen and toys, the transformation was complete. Our once-beautiful living room was now a far less attractive, but baby-friendly, environment.

Similar changes occurred throughout the house. Drawers and cupboard doors received childproof locks. Doorknob protectors barred access to "out-of-bounds" rooms to curious babies on the move — and to adults in a hurry. Feelings were easily hurt. As fall became winter, we began to feel slightly claustrophobic and displaced: "Who sits in the big corner chair?" Inanimate items took on a life of their own: "Have you seen the remote control?" Tension grew. "How old are these leftovers?" It was "too close for comfort" for me. I began to withdraw, both physically (behind the now frequently closed door) and emotionally (present but not "present").

One Carson-filled evening changed my perspective. By now an active toddler, Carson zoomed about the house, burning off his dinner. Up and down the hallway he ran. As he whizzed by me, I reached down, caught him, and "loved all over him" (which consisted of lots of loud kisses all over Carson's head, face, and neck.) Carson collapsed into a pile of giggles at my feet.

On his next round, he veered toward me

as he neared, passing tantalizingly close, as if to say, "Get me again, Grandma!" I grabbed him and again "loved him all over." This time, we both giggled uncontrollably as I set him back on his feet.

Our laughter drew the attention of Mike and Cori, who joined our game. The three of us formed a gauntlet down the hallway. As Carson dashed past, each in turn grabbed him and, to his increasing delight, covered him with kisses.

The house rang with laughter. Tears poured down our cheeks. Out of breath, I sat on the floor. It was not long before Cori and Mike joined me there.

Our new positions forced Carson to modify his strategy. Instead of running past us, he ran directly to us, throwing himself into our arms to collect kisses. Finally, he simply stood in the center of the hallway and spun. When he came to a stop, he allowed his body to drop in the general direction of the person he faced at the end of his spin. He trusted us to catch him and "love him all over" when he fell our way.

"He's playing spin the bottle," Mike exclaimed, "but he's the bottle!"

Carson's contagious joy, unmarred by the difficult circumstances, was an example to me. I looked around the small circle of family on the hallway floor. For the first time in months I didn't feel like it was "too close for comfort" but, instead, simply "close."

Life often takes sudden and surprising turns. Happiness in difficult circumstances is a moment-by-moment decision. My grandson, Carson, is helping me to create moments of happiness in every single day.

A happy heart is good medicine and a cheerful mind works healing.
Proverbs 17:22 AB

double your pleasure

Gracie Malone

I do not ask for any crown
but that which all may win.
Nor try to conquer any world
except the one within.

Louisa May Alcott

Our grandson Myles absolutely loved his pacifier. This affection . . . errr . . . this obsession lasted from a few moments after his birth until he was almost four years old. By the time he was two, the device had been lovingly dubbed his Nah Nah. The tiny plug seldom left our toddler's mouth. As the relationship between Nah Nah and Myles grew, the little tyke could actually do tricks with it. He'd look up, grin an impish grin, and, with a quick flick of his tongue, give Nah Nah a 360-degree spin without missing a beat in the sucking rhythm he had going. The antic was so darn cute that sometimes

I'd yank the pacifier out of his mouth, turn it upside down, and stick it back in just to see him twirl it right side up again.

Sometimes Myles would giggle, clamp his hand over his mouth, and run before I could get a good hold on Nah Nah's plastic ring. At other times he'd tease back, tilting his chin upward, then, quick as a wink, snap his head around so the pacifier was beyond my reach. It was a catch-me-if-you-can-but-I-really-hope-you-can kind of deal — a competitive sport that provided entertainment for the whole family.

Throughout the course of its existence, Nah Nah not only "pacified" Myles' natural sucking impulses but comforted him through many a crisis and soothed more than a few anxious moments. At bedtime the pacifier was Myles' best friend, his mama in absentia. Thus to lose his beloved Nah Nah in the middle of the night could cause a major crisis. Myles would realize the pacifier was missing, sit bolt upright in bed, howl loudly, and crawl around under the covers or on the floor until he found it and slapped it back in his mouth. He could do all this without being fully awake. My daughter-in-law Jeanna said he looked like a panic-stricken sleepwalker. Whenever a hullabaloo happened in the kid's room, she'd pull herself out of bed to help.

One unsettling night, neither Myles nor his mom could find the lost pacifier. Throughout the bedtime hours, Myles tossed and turned, making little whimpering sounds that kept everybody in the house awake. Thankfully, the very next day they located the lost device tucked deep between the sheets, and, just to insure never having to experience another "unpacified" night, Jeanna purchased a spare. Now, she thought, we're prepared for an emergency. But as soon as Myles discovered the brand-new Nah Nah, he came up with his own plan. He toddled toward bed that evening with both pacifiers in tow — one solidly plugged in his mouth and the other clutched tightly in his chubby little hand. What bliss! A suckling child with two "suckers"!

The only problem was, Myles had a hard time knowing which pacifier he loved best. Even at night, he'd plug one in, then pop it out and sample the other. Nevertheless, this delightful double dose of fun worked well until Myles matured a bit and became embarrassed — especially when sporting the two Nah Nahs in public. People would actually stop and stare when he'd remove one from his mouth, dig in his pocket for the spare, pop it between his lips, and give it the

360 twirl as he tucked the first one safely away.

Eventually, even Myles realized he had a problem. When Jeanna suggested it was time to give Nah Nah up, he was willing. One night just before bedtime they made a dramatic stop at the trashcan in the kitchen. Myles stepped on the lever and ceremoniously tossed both pacifiers inside. He strutted toward bed wearing a very grown-up smile. But after a few minutes, Jeanna heard a commotion in the kitchen. She turned on the light, and there was Myles sitting on the floor picking through the garbage like a pint-sized wino. His lips were quivering.

Jeanna couldn't bear it. She located one Nah Nah, gave it a thorough washing, and put the child to bed, where he slept peacefully. After a few more attempts, Jeanna and Myles finally conquered the problem. He tossed the remaining Nah Nah in the garbage can and left it there. For a full two weeks, the little guy hardly missed his former addiction. He was well on the way to a complete recovery when he became sick.

On the way home from the doctor's office, Myles whined and pulled on his ear as his temperature soared. When they stopped at Target to fill a prescription,

Jeanna buckled him in the shopping cart and clipped down the aisle toward the pharmacy. Suddenly Myles let out a moan that stopped the concerned mother dead in her tracks. She glanced up and spotted a huge display of pacifiers of all shapes, sizes, and colors. Myles tugged at the seat belt as he stretched toward the display. "Nahhhh, Nahhhh," he wailed. The moan came from the core of his tiny being. Then he dropped his feverish brow on the handle of the cart and wept. Jeanna couldn't resist. She bought one, opening it on the spot.

A few weeks later, Jeanna decided to address the problem again. "Myles, I've got an idea," she began. "I'm wondering if you'd like to give your Nah Nah to someone else. I'll bet there's a little boy or girl much younger than you who needs a pacifier. We could put it on the front porch and see if the tooth fairy will pick it up and deliver it to someone who really needs it."

That evening before bedtime, Jeanna located a nice gift box and stuffed it with colorful tissue. Myles gently placed his beloved Nah Nah in the folds of paper. They tied a ribbon around the box and carefully placed it on the porch. Myles strutted to bed.

Early the next morning, he ran to the porch to see what had happened. Lo and behold, the box was gone. Apparently the Nah Nah had been picked up and delivered to a needy child. Myles seemed genuinely pleased when he called me. "Gamma Gacie," he began in his very best toddler talk, "I gave Nah Nah away!" I could hear the excitement in his voice as he added, "Another little boy needed it more than me."

"I'm proud of you, Myles," I gushed. "You are so grown-up!"

Later, after Jeanna told me the whole story, I found myself thinking about Myles' courage and determination. I really was proud of him! After all, it's hard for a person — even a well-seasoned grandmother like me — to give up things that are pleasurable. Seems there is a part of us — an unmanageable toddler-like part — that longs to acquire and hang onto things we don't really need.

In a moment of self-reflection, I thought about a few of my own "Nah Nahs," like the clothes rack at Nordstrom's and the coffee shop where I drool over Grande Caramel Macchiato Latte.

I took a deep breath and marched to my bedroom closet. I picked out several outfits to give to a needy friend and a pair of shoes for my sister. I thought about a friend who

I'd invite to join me next time I visited the coffee shop. Later as I settled into bed, I felt good. For I'd been reminded of one of life's important lessons. It truly is in giving that we receive.

I have stilled and quieted myself, just as a small child is quiet with its mother. Yes, like a small child is my soul within me.
Psalm 131:2 NLT

roadkill
– it's a bonding thing

Phyllis Harmony

*May the wonder of today
be that of a child.*

Phyllis Harmony

It was my first Grandparents Day event. My five-year-old granddaughter, Aggie, was in kindergarten, and she excitedly invited me to this special celebration. I arrived early and was directed to the auditorium filled with giggles and smiling, searching faces. My little redhead jumped and waved to me from the steps where she stood with her classmates. Every grandparent was the proudest one in attendance as we listened to songs and laughed spontaneously as our grandchildren swayed with the music.

Like a gaggle of geese, we followed our little darlings to their classroom to admire various stations. One exhibited carefully printed numbers, another the alphabet, and a third was filled with family photos. Sweet little fingers pointed, and eager hands pulled their guests around the room.

As my first grandchild, Aggie got to choose the name I would be called. She chose "Ma." Not Nana or Memaw or Nonie or Grandma, just plain "Ma." I love the name and adore the voices that say it.

Aggie was excited. "Ma, let's go find the picture story I did. You're gonna love it. It's all about you and me together!" We found a ceiling-high, four-sided bulletin board at one end of the room. Aggie searched high and low for her picture. I could see that every paper had the words "Together we . . ." printed across the top, followed by a picture and a one-sentence story of something they did with their grandparent, carefully written out by the child.

With tears welling up in her twinkling brown eyes, she proclaimed, "I can't find it! Ma, it's not here, but I really did one, and it was good." Her voice trailed off in sadness and frustration. I started the grandparent search to assuage her disappointment. I looked way up to the top. There was a sweet story that read, "Grandma and I make cookies together." Another child told of playing checkers with Grandpa, and another of going to the zoo with Grandma and Grandpa.

As my eyes continued down the column, I moved a little chair and heard a squeal of delight from Aggie. "Here it is, Ma! You found it!" We squatted down together. I saw two extremely happy people in what looked like a car, smiling out the windshield. She told me that she had to use the name "Grandma" because the teacher helped her write the story. After studying the drawing, I read her account of our activity. It read: "Grandma and I look for roadkill when we are out driving together."

I looked at the picture again. Sure enough, there was a carcass beside the car. I glanced at her as she stared at me, waiting for my response. I picked her up, swung her around, and told her it was the best story in the whole class. It certainly was the most original!

I must admit, this is something we actually do together. We were driving in the country one day, and I said, "Oh, look at the roadkill!"

"What's roadkill, Ma?"

"Dead animals along the side of the road."

"Oh, hey, let's go look for more!" And we did. We've continued "the hunt" for years. I never dreamed that looking for roadkill would be such a bonding experience for us. Now little Aggie can identify just about anything by the stub of a tail.

My granddaughter is out of elementary school now, and we don't look for roadkill quite as often as we used to, but I still love to get her in a car with me for a ride. It's one of the few times I have her full attention. She has learned some of my favorite gospel songs and sings them with me, and we talk about her present and my past. I find any excuse to be with her and her bright little personality. So whether we are looking for roadkill, new clothes, or favorite snacks, one of my greatest joys is spending time with Aggie. It's a bonding thing!

Congenial conversation — what a pleasure! The right word at the right time — beautiful!
Proverbs 15:23 MSG

jesus loves the little children

Gracie Malone

Jesus loves me, this I know.
For the Bible tells me so.
Little ones to Him belong.
They are weak, but He is strong.

"Jesus Loves Me,"
Anna B. Warner (1820–1915)

Watching our little ones growing up is the most blessed experience a grandmother can have. Especially when we see them beginning to comprehend spiritual truth, making decisions that honor God, and, most importantly, developing a meaningful relationship with Jesus. The aging apostle John spoke for grandmothers everywhere when he wrote, "I have no greater joy than this, to hear of my children walking in the truth" (3 John 4 NASB).

Such a walk begins when our offspring take a good hard look at the truths they've been taught. After all, the parents' religion does not really belong to the child until he or she examines and accepts it. All three of our sons went through the painstaking process of feeling separated from God, asking questions, believing in his grace, and taking a step of faith. The experience Mike had when he was eight is especially memorable to me.

One Sunday morning, Mike seemed disturbed by the preacher's message and spent the afternoon in deep thought. Then he came to me and, in an emotional tone, said, "Mom, I'm the only one in this family that's not a Christian."

After I answered a few of his questions, our little boy asked Jesus to come into his heart. The very next Sunday he was baptized. Joe and I rejoiced, not only because Mike had found peace but also in the fact that our family circle was now 100 percent Christian.

Of course, believing in Jesus was just the first step in our children's walk toward spiritual maturity. They learned to pray and, in their own unique ways, began to relate to God on an intimate level — first as their heavenly Father and eventually as their friend.

We've also seen this remarkable transformation take place in the lives of our grand-children and other very young children. They not only become aware of God's presence at an early age but they also learn to trust him and are able to grasp deep spiritual truths. Their faith is able to see them through tough times, even some crises that would send some of us older folk into a spiritual nosedive.

Such strong faith was evident in a little girl named Jana. One day her grandmother introduced her to me in a Christian bookstore. Then she relayed the following story.

Seems Jana was only five when she had to undergo serious open-heart surgery. The little girl was apprehensive, as any one of us would be under such circumstances. But in spite of her fear, Jana showed remarkable courage and strength. She believed in Jesus, and nothing could shake her faith.

Just before the frail girl went into the operating room, she looked up at her doctor and said, "I know you are going to open up my heart."

"That's right, sweetheart," the kindly doctor replied.

"Well," Jana thought for a few moments and then added, "when you open my heart, Jesus is in there. Don't take him out."

The doctor tenderly reassured the little

girl, then turned toward the window to wipe away a stray tear and perhaps to breathe a prayer himself.

During the long, tedious procedure, Jesus stayed right there in Jana's fragile little heart — giving peace and comfort to the tiny sleeping patient. He was also present in the operating room, granting wisdom and skill to the medical team. Jana emerged from surgery with a healthy heart and has gone on to live many joyful, faith-filled years.

For I am convinced that neither death nor life, neither angels nor demons, neither the present nor the future, nor any powers, neither height nor depth, nor anything else in all creation, will be able to separate us from the love of God that is in Christ Jesus our Lord.
Romans 8:38–39

great grandma's autograph

Jeanne Zornes

More is caught than taught.

Source unknown

We never had a heavy discussion about God and life, never even prayed together outside of mealtime grace. But she left her thumbprint on my life in a way I never expected.

I called her "Grandma Neely" though there should have been a "great" in front of that name. She was the only great-grandmother I ever knew, and I knew little about her except what I noticed when she visited us and what I learned much later.

She devoted her last years to round-robin visits — a few weeks at this relative's home, then a few more weeks at another's. All welcomed her, this gentle widow whose native Norwegian tongue turned her second language, English, into gentle music.

I don't even recall who gave up a bed for Grandma Neely's visits, me or my sister. I only remember how she considered my dad's platform rocker, upholstered in fifties-style red tapestry, her rightful place to sit. She'd stay there for hours, her worn black leather Bible in her lap or resting on the lamp table and her needles clicking in rhythm on another knitting project. Sometimes the needles were silent, and her eyes were closed. I never knew if she was napping or praying.

One day I decided I wanted her signature in my new red-covered autograph book. I'd gotten it for my tenth birthday and already my friends had signed its pastel pages. Oh, the things little girls write:

"Two in a car, two little kisses, two weeks later, Mr. and Mrs."

"When you get old and think you're sweet, take off your shoes and smell your feet."

"Can you sign my autograph book, Grandma Neely?" I asked as I knelt beside her. She put aside her knitting and smiled, her pale blue eyes sparkling behind her glasses.

"I'll come back a little later," I promised. I wanted to give her enough time to recall a fantastic autograph ditty. With seventy-some years of life, she surely knew the best.

I'll never forget what she wrote. The meaning behind her carefully chosen autograph impacted me in a profound way. There, in her precise European script, was her name. And she had signed it under the sixteen words of 3 John 4: "I have no greater joy than to hear that my children are walking in the truth."

Years later, while working on our family history, I realized how her character was forged in suffering and faith. She came to America as a small child. Soon her father died of flu contracted on the voyage. Her mother remarried another Norwegian; then she died of tuberculosis. Her stepfather remarried, giving Grandma Neely double stepparents.

As an adult, Grandma Neely outlived two husbands. She opened her home to those in need, including a granddaughter who was the oldest of nine born to an impoverished Montana farmer and wife. She invited this young woman to come to Washington State and live with her and attend college — to get a better start in life. When that granddaughter married, Grandma Neely served as "mother of the bride." Now I understood the close relationship my mother — that granddaughter — had with her.

My memories of Grandma Neely were always connected to her well-used Bible. As a child, I wondered if I'd ever comprehend the Bible well enough to consider it my lifeline to God.

I got another glimpse of her faith just months before her death. My family was visiting her in a nursing home after her stroke. She struggled to communicate, but I understood this much: "I was on the Glory Road. I saw Jesus, but he wouldn't let me go on."

A few months later, she finished her journey on the "Glory Road." But relatives never forgot her. One family member reported that Grandma Neely for years fasted and prayed once a week for her descendants. Dozens of people — including me — had their names and spiritual needs lifted to God in prayer.

A couple of decades later, my grandmother and my own parents died within a couple years of one another. By then, I'd acutely sensed the torch of faith passed on to my generation, along with the need to pray for certain extended family members. Somehow, I wanted Grandma Neely to know her prayers for me were not in vain.

In the task of dissolving my parents' belongings, I came across my little autograph book, left at home in a pile of mementos. I opened its now-weathered red cover and smiled to read the silly ditties from friends. Then I turned with reverence to Great-Grandma Neely's page.

Once again my eyes fell on Grandma's perfect European script, where she had signed her name, like a prophetic commission, under the verse I had read years earlier: "I have no greater joy than to hear that my children are walking in the truth."

Her quiet witness was still influencing my life.

Those who are wise will shine like the brightness of the heavens, and those who lead many to righteousness, like the stars for ever and ever.
Daniel 12:3

just among friends

Gracie Malone

Count your age by friends — not years; count your life by smiles — not tears.

Friendship

My grandmother, Mama, was a dignified woman with roots that grew deep into the soil of Southern Baptist fundamentalism. This Christian woman would never, and I do mean never, say or do anything that could be considered crude or even slightly off color. In fact, if a conversation took on even the slightest sexual innuendo, and she found it the least bit funny, Mama would cup her hand over her mouth so nobody could tell she was grinning. (At least she thought we couldn't tell!) Because she was so straightlaced, we were all surprised when we heard about an incident that happened in the nursing home where she lived out the last few years of her life.

Our "Mama" could almost always be found in the facility's living room with a circle of friends sitting around listening as she spun a tale or talked of days gone by. Every morning she'd climb into her wheelchair, propel herself down the hall — using a weird but highly effective combination of hand and foot movements — and edge her way into whatever conversation was taking place at the time. Sometimes she would join in a game of dominoes or help the other residents put together a puzzle. Mama would do almost anything to be in the mainstream of nursing home society.

While Mama loved being the life of the party, she tired easily, especially once she became ninety. But her physical limitations were no problem for our feisty grandma. When she needed to rest, she could easily find her way back to her room. For as long as she had been in the nursing home, she'd lived on the east wing, third door on the left side of the hall, and occupied the bed on the right side of the room.

Unfortunately, after Mama had lived in the nursing home several years, we noticed that she was becoming more and more senile.

In the midst of this difficulty, the facility was refurbished, and Mama was moved to another room in the west wing. The east wing became the men's dormitory and two gentlemen took up residence in Mama's old quarters. The move was more than a little disconcerting to my grandmother.

Nevertheless she continued to make daily jaunts down the hall, into the living room, and somehow got back to her new location. But one morning on her way back to her room, she had a serious lapse of memory. In a troubling turn of events, she ended up in her old room, parked her wheelchair, and . . . climbed in bed with the man who now occupied her former space.

Apparently the old fellow she warmed up to was of sounder mind than our gregarious grandmother. For he told on Mama, suggesting to the nursing staff that my grandmother had acted in a . . . well . . . flirtatious manner.

This kind of news travels fast even in a place where everything else moves slowly. Before long, we found out all about Mama's misadventure. As the story goes, she had snuggled up close to the gentleman, looked into his cloudy blue eyes, and spoke in a passionate tone: "Papa, at our age, I don't think we should have more than two kids."

As family members have passed this story down through the years since Mama's homegoing, some of us have snickered and blushed and a few have become angry at the nursing home staff who caused Mama's confusion in the first place. But whenever I hear the story retold, I can't help but smile. Mama lived long and brought us joy and laughter to the very end of her life. I hope I can do the same for my grandchildren.

A good life gets passed on to the grandchildren.
Proverbs 13:22 MSG

the blue ford

Laura Leathers

*A pint of example
is worth a barrelful of advice.*

Author unknown

"Honk! Honk!" the blue Ford blared as it approached our driveway. This was my grandmother's way of informing me I was late for Sunday school when she did not see me standing in my usual place, next to our gigantic silver mailbox.

"Bye, Mom," I yelled as I bolted out our front door. Rarely was Grandma early. Therefore I felt justified waiting inside because there was no sense standing outside next to the dirt road until I knew she was coming. I also knew that I could be out the door and in her car before she came to a full stop. Once I was situated in the front seat, off she would go, taking on the winding one-lane country dirt road as if she owned it.

The blue eight-cylinder stick shift Ford Fairlane was at her beck and call. She put it into first gear just long enough to take the first major curve to the right. With her foot on the clutch she shifted quickly into third gear, and off we would fly. Down the big hill, across the bridge, up and down another hill, and then she would slow down just enough to take a sharp curve to the left. It was a straight shot to the church after that. Only one stop sign could slow us down. Grandma would simply look to the left over the corn in the field, and if no cars were coming, she kept on going. Ahhh, I loved her sense of adventure.

A few minutes later Grandma parked the blue Ford by the side door of the century-old LaMarsh Creek Baptist Church. It was my job to help Grandma get her "stuff" out of the car. Once I had her items properly placed on the desk, I would hurry to my class where Mrs. Nowack had her flannel board and pictures ready for the lesson. How I loved that woman! She could tell the best stories from the Bible.

After class it was back upstairs to the small sanctuary where I sat next to Grandma for the church services. Little did I realize how much she was shaping my future. She showed me how to hold a hymnal, sing with gusto, and place my offering in the plate. I watched her open the large black-bound Bible, mark the date and the pastor's name next to the text he was reading, and then take notes on the back of an old envelope she pulled from her purse.

Week after week, year after year, my Grandma and I repeated this procedure. My two younger sisters joined us when they reached the age of five. Looking back, I realize Grandma and her blue Ford not only took me to church but also to the Ladies' Quilting Bee, ice-cream socials, visits to church members, and to vacation Bible school. She was shaping my spiritual development. She taught me the importance of being at church and with God's people. Every place she took me was another opportunity for me to hear the Word of God and to connect with other Christians.

After Grandma died, her belongings were dispersed among relatives. I have to admit I was a little disappointed when I received my box of items. It was all the leftovers that no one else wanted. However, I now realize that God gave me exactly what I needed to remember how Grandma had influenced my life. Among the items I received were several of her teacups that have become a part of my collection, and they are used in ministry. But the greatest treasure of all was her Bible. It even had a few of her bookmarks and old envelopes inside. I recently discovered that this Bible was given to her in April 1959. That year I was five years old, the age she started taking me to church.

Grandma and I spent many hours together over the years, and we had glorious adventures as we traveled in her blue Ford. However, nothing compares to the adventures I have found and the treasures I have discovered as I study my Bible each day. I'm thankful I had a grandma who demonstrated the importance of studying God's Word and being in church.

Recently I opened her Bible and there, on the left side of the aged white paper, she had written the following verse: "He that dwelleth in the secret place of the most High shall abide under the shadow of the Almighty. . . . He is my refuge and my fortress: my God; in him will I trust" (Psalm 91:1–2 KJV).

I realized Grandma was still teaching me to trust in the absolute truth of his Word.

Your word is a lamp to my feet
and a light for my path.
Psalm 119:105

sandwich-to-go

Gracie Malone

If you want to hear God laugh,
tell Him your plans!

Jeanette Clift George

When I answered the phone, I quickly recognized the soft, ever-so-slightly trembling voice of my mom. "Gracie, I think I broke my toe. I was getting something out of the freezer and when I let go of my walker, it fell forward and hit right on the big one. It's black and blue and swollen. I can't even wear my shoe. But you don't have to come over. I've already doctored it with Campho-Phenique."

I couldn't help smiling as I hung up the phone. As far as my mother is concerned, camphorated oil can cure most anything, and what it can't fix, mentholated cream can. Her idea of a well-stocked medicine cabinet is a roll of cotton, a bottle of

161

Campho-Phenique, Vick's salve, and a ChapStick. These few items have served her well for as long as I can remember, keeping her little body well greased and operating efficiently for nearly a century. It's hard to argue with success.

Even though she'd said not to come, I could tell Mom really needed a visit from the one she still calls her "baby girl." Besides, I wanted to see for myself how serious her injuries were. I jumped in my car and headed to her house thirty minutes away. Once there, I took off her sock and removed the oily ball of cotton to assess the damage. The toe was exactly as she'd described — bruised and swollen. But she could wiggle it, so I decided her home remedies would take care of the situation. I soaked the cotton with a fresh libation of oil and gently replaced her soft white sock. While she relaxed in her recliner, her foot nestled on a fluffy embroidered pillow, I warmed soup for her supper and vacuumed the living room. Then I kissed her good-bye and headed back home.

When I pulled in our driveway, I realized it was time for me to switch roles. I was no longer my mother's "baby girl." I was "Grandma Gracie" to the six kids playing in our backyard. In a "senior moment," I'd forgotten they were coming over to swim and roast hot dogs. As I parked and exited my car, the kids came a-running, throwing their wet little arms around me, slathering my cheeks with sloppy kisses.

Now I'll admit, it takes a grandma to love it. But love it I do! As I stood surrounded by all that affection, I felt a fresh burst of energy stirring deep within my tired frame. Like an Energizer Bunny with brand-new batteries, I whirled around and headed for the kitchen to start supper. Five-year-old Mary followed close behind.

"Grandma Gracie, can I have some chocolate milk?" she began as she opened the pantry door and shuffled through the shelves looking for the Nestlé's Quik. "Pleeeeeze, can I? Grandma Gracie, I'm dying!" I started to hand over the milk, thus not only saving the child's life but assuring my place as World's Nicest Grandma, when I glanced out the window, eyed her parents, and decided to do the mature thing. Knowing they would not approve such a sugary concoction before dinner, I said no. Mary begged. I felt compelled to stick with my answer.

The decision did not set well with Mary. With her hands firmly planted on her hips, she huffed out of the kitchen, marched right into my bedroom, and called 911.

Imagine me trying to explain to the dispatcher, "There's no problem here. No, sir, . . . except, well, I have six grandkids over here for supper and I wouldn't serve a chocolate milk appetizer."

As thy days, so shall thy strength be.
Deuteronomy 33:25 KJV

sharing grandchildren

Linda Neff

*We make a living by what we get;
we make a life by what we give.*

Duane Hulse

The same year my mother turned eighty, she was scheduled for hip surgery. A few days later I was allowed to take my four young children to the hospital for a brief visit. She was prepared.

After a long retirement following thirty years of teaching, the impulse to instruct never left her. When getting her things ready for the hospital stay, she had included a diagram of her surgical procedure. After our arrival, she produced it with enthusiasm from the bedside drawer. Carefully she explained to her grandchildren what the surgeon had done.

Next she dug into the same drawer and pulled out candy for the children. It had obviously been placed there in anticipation of their visit. Then my mother lifted the sheet from her leg and displayed her long bandage. Their eyes were wide with wonder. The bandage was so much larger than the ones that came out of the Band-Aid boxes for their small cuts and scrapes.

"Now," she whispered, "go to the next bed and say hello to Betty, my roommate. She doesn't get many visitors. Remember, older people love the touch of young unwrinkled skin, so be sure to take her hand."

I had never heard of someone sharing her hospital visitors with another patient. Betty, mother's roommate, was delighted with her enthusiastic young visitors.

How like my mother, I thought, to teach her grandchildren how to be compassionate in the middle of her own hospitalization. I quickly realized my mother was still teaching me, by example, how to demonstrate acts of kindness that make people feel valued, loved, and significant.

My children are almost grown now, and when I see them graciously reach out to others with compassion, I smile, knowing the gift of compassion has been passed to the next generation by a loving grandmother.

Dress in the wardrobe God picked out for you: compassion, kindness, humility, quiet strength, discipline. . . . And regardless of what else you put on, wear love. It's your basic, all-purpose garment. Never be without it.

Colossians 3:12, 14 MSG

long-distance grandmothers

Gracie Malone

*If nothing is going well,
call your grandmother.*

Italian proverb

What would we do without a telephone? It connects us to our grandchildren, some of whom live long distances from their doting grandparents. Even those who live close by seem to open up and talk more freely with a handset pressed against their tiny ears.

As soon as my grandbabies learned to talk they developed an affinity for the phone, and, according to my daughters-in-law, would jump up and down excitedly whenever they got a call from their Grandma Gracie.

My grandson Connor seemed especially captivated by this manner of communication. When he was barely three, he would parade around the room with the receiver

over his shoulder mimicking the manner-
isms of his dad, who could usually be found
talking on his cell phone as he puttered
around in the garage. At other times,
Connor would sprawl on a chair, his tiny
legs draped over the arm like a self-absorbed
teen. I could hear him announce, as he
cupped his hand over the mouthpiece, "It's
for me. Please be quiet! It's Grandma
Gracie."

Connor knew if he needed an extra dose
of love and encouragement, he could usually count on his Grandma Gracie to come
up with just the right words. *Usually!* One
time, when Connor called, I, being a bit
preoccupied, didn't respond with my usual
good cheer.

I was particularly busy when he phoned to
relay some good news. "Grandma Gracie,"
he began, "I can swim . . . all the way across
the pool."

"Really?"

"Yep . . . all the way across, without my
water wings."

My response time must have been a bit
too slow, my tone a tad nonchalant, for I
overheard his muffled voice as he cupped
his hand over the mouthpiece and muttered, "Dad, she didn't say 'That's great!' "

Until that moment, I hadn't realized that

I'd treated his good news in a less-than-enthusiastic manner. Nor did I realize how routinely I'd said those words — "That's great!" Feeling a bit chagrined, I quickly tried to correct my error. "Connor," I yelled, "wait just a minute. Did you say you swam *all the way* across the pool? *Without* water wings? That's great, Connor! *Just great!*"

"Oh, thanks!" he answered. I know it isn't possible, but I actually thought I could *hear* his big grin as he handed the receiver to his dad.

Unfortunately, this wasn't the only time I almost blew it with my young grandson.

One morning the phone rang persistently. When I answered, I thought I recognized the voice of our older grandson, Luke. "Hey, Luke," I chirped.

"No!" a tiny voice on the other end of the line came back in a perturbed tone. "It's me." Suddenly I realized my mistake and, like a kitten falling off the back of a chair, figured out a way to land on my feet.

"Of course it's you, Connor. It's just that . . . well . . . your voice sounded so grown-up. I guess I thought it was someone much older."

"Well, you've got that exactly right," Connor said confidently.

170

Thankfully, Connor and I have managed to maintain a close relationship in spite of my verbal goofs.

It wasn't a week after the aforementioned mistake when he sauntered into the kitchen in his pajamas and handed his mom the telephone. "Call Grandma Gracie," he begged. "I have *sooo* many things I want to say to her."

I'm glad Connor knows that in spite of my blunders, I really care about the details of his everyday life.

Gently encourage the stragglers, and reach out for the exhausted, pulling them to their feet. Be patient, . . . attentive to individual needs. . . . Look for the best in each other, and always do your best to bring it out. Be cheerful no matter what. . . . This is the way God wants you who belong to Christ Jesus to live.
1 Thessalonians 5:14–18 MSG

caught on film!

Ginger Kamps

Prayer is not overcoming God's reluctance; it is laying hold of His highest willingness.

Richard Chenevix

My daughter Traci called me on the phone, her voice trembling. She was crying. "Mom!" she blurted out between sobs. "The test was negative. I am not pregnant!"

Traci and Kevin had been married two years, and they had been trying to conceive for several months to no avail. Traci was sure this time was it. But the in-home pregnancy test told her otherwise.

What a disappointment! My heart broke for my daughter, and I tried to find words to console her. "Oh, I am so sorry, honey. Don't be upset. It will happen in God's perfect timing," I said, trying to be optimistic and upbeat.

"But I was sure I was pregnant this time,

and now the test says I'm not," Traci cried. "I want to have a baby!" Her heartfelt sobs broke my heart, and I cried with her.

"Well, honey," I said bravely, "keep praying. We will just have to trust God for positive results next time."

We hung up the phone, and I went to my prayer room, our home library. Lined with bookshelves on three walls, it smells of leather and wood. Beneath the window sits an old oak library table and standing next to it is a solid oak chair where I placed a genuine made-in-Israel Jewish prayer shawl. I had given it to my mother as a gift, and when she passed away, it came back to me. The oak chair became my altar that day as I knelt in prayer to seek God on behalf of my barren daughter.

As I called out to God, tears rolled down my cheeks. Traci was my firstborn. I had miscarried my second child, and my son, Perry, was my third. I had become a mother at a young age and had no trouble conceiving, so I hadn't experienced my daughter's pain.

That day a Scripture I had memorized came back to me: "We do not know what we ought to pray for, but the Spirit himself intercedes for us with groans that words cannot express" (Romans 8:26). I struggled for the words to pray for my daughter. As I agonized in my communication with God that day, my words, emotions, and fervent cries were sent heavenward as I pleaded with him to grant my daughter's request for a child.

Two weeks later, Traci called again. "Mom," she said with a lilt in her voice, "I went to the pregnancy center and had a pregnancy test. I'm pregnant!"

Several weeks later Traci had her first ultrasound, and she joyously brought the pictures over to show my husband, Kenny, and me. I had become ill very suddenly that day and was sleeping when she brought the picture into the bedroom. I could barely raise my head and, between half-closed eyes, I groggily looked at the little piece of black and white paper she was clutching in her hand. I was trying hard to see the outline of a baby in the picture, but it just wasn't registering. Traci said, "Look closer, Mom. Do you see it?"

I looked again and saw an arrow and a letter of the alphabet next to dark and light shadows. Now it was becoming clearer. There were two letters of the alphabet with arrows, an "A" and a "B." Traci once again said, "Do you see it?" her voice growing with impatience. There they were — not one baby, but two babies were in her womb! I sat straight up in my bed, finally understanding that my first grandbaby would actually be two! Joy flooded the room!

We thought back on the time line and realized that when Traci had called with the negative result of the first pregnancy test, she was, in fact, very early in her pregnancy. We believe that my fervent prayer for her that day may have caused the egg to split and become two identical little twin girls. Every day I thank God for allowing me to be "Grandma Ginger" to the beautiful grandchildren he brought into my life. Those precious babies, once "caught on film" in their mother's womb, are my crowning joy!

Children's children
are a crown to the aged.
Proverbs 17:6

all creatures small

Gracie Malone

All Creatures great and small . . .
The Lord God made them all.

"All Things Bright and Beautiful,"

Cecil F. Alexander (1818–95)

My sister Lois's great-grandson, Ashton, three, is what we older folks refer to as "all boy." That means he loves dirt, sticks, rocks, and anything else that relates to the great outdoors — including four-footed creatures and bugs. One afternoon, Lois called to tell me the following story.

Ashton came running into his grandma's house with a big smile on his face and his little hand clenched into a tiny fist. "Grandma, guess what I've got in my hand!" He extended his arm in Lois's direction. He unfolded his fingers and proudly showed off his latest discovery — a tiny, gray, multi-jointed creature known in Texas as a "roly-poly" bug. The little bug had rolled itself into a tiny ball no bigger than a BB with its hairy legs tucked inside.

As Ashton held it forward on his palm, the little creature suddenly fell to the floor, where it unrolled and started crawling across the carpet. Ashton got down on his hands and knees, crawled alongside it for a while, and then watched the little bug creep toward his grandma's chair. After a few minutes, he picked it up, brought his hand close to his mouth and spoke tenderly, "Where are you going, little roly-poly?" With eyes shining, he turned toward his grandma, then, since she didn't appear squeamish at all, he dropped the tiny bug into her palm.

As Lois sat there cradling the tiny creature, her mind flooded with memories, including days when she was a little girl with little else to play with than the creatures in her backyard. "When I was growing up, I played with roly-poly bugs too," she explained. Then she told Ashton about coaxing doodlebugs out of their cone-shaped home in the sand, putting lightning bugs in a jar where she could watch their fluorescent glow cast an eerie light through the glass container. She remembered tying a string around the middle of an old locust and hearing its loud humming as it flew in circles overhead, like a tiny tethered airplane. Lois paused before adding, "I played with ladybugs too."

That sparked something in Ashton's little mind. "Poppie and G.G. have ladybugs in their backyard!" Sure enough, Lois remembered when her son and daughter-in-law, with Ashton's help, had created a flowerbed for Texas wildflowers. They purchased a large quantity of ladybugs from a garden catalog to release in that bed to help control harmful insects. Ashton loved to watch the ladybugs spread their red dotted wings and fly from one bloom to another.

Later that evening Lois took another jaunt down memory lane, stopping to recall the days when one of her own little boys — Jerry, Tommy, or Larry — would run in the house after playing outside in their big backyard. She recalled the musty smell of dirt and sweat, the salty kisses on their foreheads, the dirty fingernails from digging in the sandbox, that ring of dust we called "grandma's beads" caught in the wrinkles of their neck, and little roly-poly bugs clenched in their fists.

"You know, Gracie," Lois said, "even though years come and go and generations multiply, some things never change. And it's the little things in life that bring us the greatest joy."

I look up at your macro-skies, dark and enormous, your handmade sky-jewelry, Moon and stars mounted in their settings. Then I look at my micro-self and wonder, Why do you bother with us? . . . Yet . . . You put us in charge of your handcrafted world, repeated to us your Genesis-charge, Made us lords of sheep and cattle, even animals out in the wild, Birds flying and fish swimming, whales singing in the ocean deeps. God, brilliant Lord, your name echoes around the world.
Psalm 8:3–9 MSG

www.grandma.com

Bonnie Afman Emmorey

*The real trick is to stay alive
as long as you live.*

Ann Landers

They had little in common, but they connected. It started about ten years ago. Jordan was in his early teens. Grandma was in her early seventies. Jordan was one of the finest cross-country runners in the state of Michigan. Grandma did water aerobics with "old people." Jordan loved fast food and soda. Grandma made the equivalent of a Thanksgiving dinner on a daily basis. Jordan loved cappuccino and lattes. Grandma drank one cup of decaf a day. Jordan made straight A's in school. Grandma made puzzles.

When the Internet became available to the masses, my mother thought she was too old to learn anything new, yet she took to it like a teenager. Jordan *was* a teenager. Over the next few years, new topics of conversation emerged. From fonts to servers and everything in between, Jordan and Grandma connected. When Grandma had a fatal error appear on her screen, Jordan was her first call. Jordan said, "Grandma, you need to take a basic computer class. You would learn so much and feel more confident."

Grandma was not excited. "I'm too old. My brain can't possibly take in and remember anything so technical."

"Wait just a minute, Grandma. Your brain is just like a computer that has had so much information put into it that it feels like it might crash. Don't worry! It won't! It just needs to be organized and filed properly, and it might take you a bit longer to pull up certain information, but you definitely still have access to everything. You're a top-of-the-line model! But remember, when I leave for college, I won't be as available to fix your computer glitches." He was confident that Grandma, even at her advanced age, would benefit from going back to school. And she did.

Jordan made many six-hour round trips to Grandma's house to work with her and her computer. She became gifted at creating unique and special greeting cards made especially for the recipient. She would communicate daily with friends and family through email.

When she upgraded to a new computer, Jordan rejoiced with her. One Christmas, Jordan and his brother bought Grandma the best printer they could find, better than either of them had themselves. They were more excited about giving that one gift and watching her open it than about opening their own presents.

As I watched that scene, my heart rejoiced as I thought of all the time Jordan spent with Grandma and how important she had become to him. I had always been jealous of my friends who had their parents living in the same town with them, ready to babysit and spend time with their grandchildren. Who would have guessed that my son would develop such a close relationship with a grandmother who had always lived hours away? When Jordan left for Columbia University in New York City, I was amazed when he made spending time with Grandma a priority during his brief visits home.

She still calls him when she has a computer glitch, and he continues to help her fix minor problems. Grandma now has Jordan's cell phone number in her speed dial.

Jordan thinks it's time for Grandma to get her *own* cell phone. Who would have thought they would have so much in common?

Look for the best in each other,
and always do your best to bring it out.
1 Thessalonians 5:15 MSG

life's little bloopers

Gracie Malone

A closed mouth gathers no foot.

Found on a sign in front of a church

I wish I could say that my tongue has become a bit more silver, now that I'm easing into the golden years, but, alas, I still manage to get myself into hot water now and then. Just recently, I meant to ask a guy at church if he was able to rest on his day off, but instead I asked, "So, on your day off, do you sleep around?" When my hubby let out an audible gasp, I realized what I'd said and stammered, "Oh, I meant lay around and sleep. Then I quickly added, "Oh, never mind! None of this is my business. Don't answer that question."

Such verbal goof-ups leave me red-faced and feeling more than a little bit dumb. I know I'm not alone in my penchant for verbal mismanagement, for just the other day my friend Carolyn reminded me of a blooper she made when she was a student at Texas A & M University.

Seems it was blistering hot in her student apartment, and she was strapped for cash. Carolyn knew if she turned the air conditioner on, she'd have a hard time paying her electric bill, so she grabbed her brand-new, yet-to-be-used Sears credit card, jumped in her car, and drove into town to purchase a fan. When she burst through the store's front door, she spotted a nice-looking college student clerk and blurted out her request. "Hey," she began lightheartedly, "do you have any ovulating fans?" The guy didn't even blush as he replied, "I think they're called oscillating fans and they're right over there." Carolyn grabbed one, paid for it, and made a mad dash out of there.

Such bloopers are not limited to the older generation or even to the female gender. But somehow when the youngest members of our families commit verbal blunders, it's a whole lot cuter or funnier than when we seasoned female saints do.

My brother Charles told me about one incident that happened with his ten-year-old grandson on the way home from a funeral with his parents. He was quiet for several minutes, apparently deeply impacted by what he's seen and heard.

"Granddad," Colt began in a thoughtful tone, "I guess everybody has to die sooner or later."

Charles took a deep breath, wondering what he could say to make the whole experience a bit easier for his curious preteen grandson to handle. "Yep, dying is part of living I guess. Are you worried about it?"

"Not really," Colt continued, "but I've figured out one thing. When I die, I don't want to be buried in the ground. I just want to be castrated and put in a bottle."

Later, thinking about this funny story, I remembered an incident that happened when our son Mike was in first grade. My next-door neighbor Barbara was driving the car pool. Running a little bit late and feeling flustered, she whipped into the parking lot of Bowie School and yelled, "Hurry up, kids, you're going to be late."

The other children grabbed their books and started to run, but Mike froze. Apparently his teacher had already warned the students in her class about being tardy. Barbara glanced in her rearview mirror and saw Mike gripping the back of the seat, a stricken look on his little face. "Oh, no," he moaned, "I sure hope I'm not retarded."

This is the same kid who, as an outspoken eight-year-old, issued a warning to me about my fast-paced lifestyle. "Mom," he chided, "you really live life in the Vaseline!" When I heard that, I promised, right then and there, to slow down a bit. After all, life in the slippery "Vaseline" is bound to sooner or later result in a collision.

To those of you, both young and old, who are troubled as I am with "foot in mouth disease," let's be thankful for friends who can see past our words and into our hearts. And perhaps, before we reach our final resting place beneath the sod (or in a bottle), we will have learned to keep our mouths shut.

When there are many words,
transgression is unavoidable,
but he who restrains his lips is wise.
Proverbs 10:19 NASB

friends with god

Gracie Malone

Dear God, I think about you sometimes,
even when I'm not praying. Love, Elliott

Author unknown, Internet

I love the sincere, no-nonsense prayers of children. Even though most of them have never taken a course on how to pray or memorized a single prayer promise from the Bible, they can teach us older folk a thing or two about talking to God.

Children have no problem being thorough in their prayers. They are quite comfortable sharing every detail with their heavenly Father, especially when they're expressing thanks. When our son Matt took his turn offering the blessing at mealtimes, the dialog usually went something like this: "Thank you, God, for the mashed potatoes, and gravy, and . . . Mmm . . . the corn, and the bread and butter. And . . . most of all for the dessert. (What's for dessert, Mom? Chocolate pudding?) Thanks for the chocolate pudding and, uhhh . . . the Cool Whip. (Do we have any Cool Whip, Mom?) Amen."

I've also noticed that children are not timid when it comes to asking for God's blessing. When it came time for bedtime prayers, our son Mike mentioned everybody in our family, our circle of friends, and all sorts of spiritual and national leaders. Matt was usually the one to put the caboose on Mike's endless train of "God blesses" by jumping in with a hearty and heartfelt "Amen."

And I'm not the only matriarch who's been pleasantly surprised at the way her offspring present their requests. They seem to have no problem identifying their needs and asking God to take care of them. My friend Anita told me how her granddaughter, Katie, taught her to be specific in her prayers. Katie is a sensitive little girl with special needs. She loves babies, but simply cannot endure their crying.

One day when Anita was babysitting her four-month-old grandson, Cade, the baby was especially cranky. As the evening progressed, he burst into tears several times. And every time the baby cried, Katie tuned up too. "Please make him stop crying," Katie whimpered. "Why is Cade so unhappy?"

Anita had her hands full. She would bounce the baby, then wipe Katie's tears, bounce the baby and wipe Katie's tears. Finally, Cade quieted down and Anita pulled Katie onto her lap. "Cade isn't sad or unhappy, sweetheart," she patiently explained, "he cries because he feels uncomfortable, wants a bottle, or needs his diaper changed. You know, babies can't talk, so when they need something they just cry."

Katie seemed to understand, but she still didn't like it. When the baby finally went to sleep and Katie was ready for bed, the little girl knelt to say her prayers. "Dear Lord," she began fervently, "puh-leeeze help Cade learn to talk!"

Perhaps the most important aspect of prayer is simply recognizing God's presence and relating to him with spontaneity and freedom. It's a concept our little grandson Luke was able to grasp at an early age.

Luke and his little brother, Connor, were visiting with me while their mom and dad took a weekend trip. Early one morning, the boys stumbled into the living room and climbed in my lap for a hug. As we rocked back and forth in my chair, rays of bright sunshine filtered through the open shutters, bounced off the prism hanging in my kitchen window, and cast rainbows of brilliant color on the white walls. When Luke spotted the rainbows, he rubbed his eyes, slipped out of my chair, and stood transfixed for a moment. Then with a flash of insight and in a tone that reflected reverence and awe, he announced, "Grandma Gracie, God is here!"

Connor wiggled out of my lap, and both little boys began jumping up and down in the sparkling light, making a myriad of colors dance across their faces. As they laughed and danced in the bright sunshine, I felt God's presence too.

Not long after this spiritual experience, Luke decided he'd tired of saying a memorized prayer. He was ready to talk to God in his own words. One night he and his daddy (the aforementioned Matt) talked about it. "God is your friend, Luke," Matt began. "You can say anything you want to him."

Luke quickly understood the concept. Later that evening when they knelt together beside the bed, Luke talked freely, like a child talking to a good friend that he trusted and loved. Then he concluded his prayer with, "Good-bye, Jesus, have a nice day."

I have called you friends, for everything that I learned from my Father I have made known to you.
John 15:15

who's the boss?

Carol Kent

Life is no brief candle to me. It is sort of a splendid torch, which I have got hold of for a moment, and I want to make it burn as brightly as possible before handing it on to future generations.

George Bernard Shaw

We were nearing the end of Thanksgiving weekend, and my husband and I were visiting our son and his family in Florida. After preparing multiple meals of leftover turkey and mashed potatoes, all of us were ready for a change of menu. Hannah, age eight, volunteered to go with me on a run to Taco Bell.

Ah, I thought. This time alone with Hannah will give me an opportunity to let her know how precious she is to me, and I might get a chance to find out where she's coming from spiritually at this time in her life.

Waiting at a red light, I queried, "Hannah, have you thought about what you want to be when you grow up?"

"Yes," she quickly responded. "I want to be a movie star so I can make a million bucks!"

"What would you do with that much money?" I asked.

She needed no extra time for thoughtful consideration of how to spend her fortune. "I'd buy me a Hummer!"

The speed of her response surprised me, so I immediately asked, "What would you do with a vehicle that big?"

Without pausing for air, she said, "Oh, Grammy, I'd pick up all of the lost and hurt dogs and take care of them."

I was struck with her obvious compassion and with the thought she had put into her response. This was a subject she had considered long before I asked the question. Still, I wanted to go deeper and discover what she was thinking about her destiny and about her relationship with the Lord. "Hannah, what do you think you would like to do for God when you grow up?"

Crossing her arms with a bit of defiance, she looked at me with conviction and stated emphatically: "I think I would like to be him, because then I could be the boss of me!"

I didn't have an immediate comeback because her reply took me by surprise. Before long she was singing out loud in the passenger seat and within minutes we were ordering our take-out dinner. We soon returned home with our arms filled with tacos, burritos, and nachos, and we enjoyed a lively family meal together.

Later I thought about Hannah's namesake in the Bible — a woman with a strong desire for a son, who believed God would grant her request. Hannah prayed. God answered. And the course of history was changed. I wondered how my strong-willed Hannah would change the course of history. My thoughts turned into a prayer as I pondered that important conversation with my granddaughter:

"Lord, thank you for placing Hannah in my life. Her personality is enthusiastic, vibrant, and alive. She makes me laugh out loud at unexpected moments. Her will is strong and her responses are not always what I expect. I know you have a powerful work to do in her heart. Help me to be sensitive to her questions and wise with my responses. Lord, I pray that you will mold her will to yours and that she will soon discover the greatest joy comes in letting you be in charge of her life!"

That holiday weekend visit has been a constant reminder of the importance of praying for my granddaughters. I think it's the most important job I have!

I desire to do your will, O my God;
your law is within my heart.
Psalm 40:8

from the heart

Gracie Malone

You really shouldn't say, "I love you," unless you mean it. But if you mean it, you should say it a lot. People forget.

Anonymous eight-year-old

One day after school, five-year-old Montana gathered a few pieces of red construction paper, a lace paper doily, plastic scissors, and a handful of markers. Then he began working on what seemed to be a rather complicated project. Seated at the kitchen table, he cut and pasted, colored with the markers, and occasionally wiped his forehead with the back of his hand. Obviously he was creating a valentine. His mother tried not to be conspicuous as she observed, not wanting to spoil her child's surprise.

Finally, Montana completed the project and asked for an envelope. Jeanna located an unused card envelope and pretended not to notice as her son slipped his handmade expression of love inside. He picked up the black marker, then with a satisfied expression on his upturned face, sweetly asked, "Mom, how do you spell Mrs. Wray?"

Suddenly Jeanna understood the valentine was *not* for her, but for Montana's kindergarten teacher. A flush of emotion swept over her as she realized her son was growing up. The reality hit hard. Montana's world was enlarging to include other adults that he respected — and loved.

On one hand, Jeanna was pleased about her son's social growth, especially when she thought about the child's sensitivity and thoughtfulness. But she also felt like she was losing something precious. No longer was she the exclusive source of her son's childhood training. Her thoughts took a leap forward, and she wondered if there would come a time when Montana would value his teacher's instruction more than his mother's. She also realized there would be other women in her little boy's life — some that he would love deeply. Then, like a video on fast-forward, she imagined a scene that portrayed Montana as an independent, self-sufficient young man, and she felt a deep sense of gratitude.

Turning toward the window she brushed away a tear that had spilled over onto her cheek. Jeanna didn't want Montana to see this display of emotion.

But Montana had noticed! The lad jumped up from his place at the table and rushed to his mother's side. Putting his arms around her waist he hugged her tightly and said, "Mom, I love you more than anybody in the whole world."

Jeanna slipped her arms around her son's tiny shoulders. "I love you, too, sweetheart."

After a few moments of silence, Montana took a deep breath and spoke with amazing perception and depth. "Mom, you have my *real* heart. I'm just giving Mrs. Wray a copy."

When Jeanna told me this story, it reminded me that God, our heavenly Parent, wants his children to love him wholeheartedly too. Sometimes the children of God get the wrong idea. We think we can divide up our affections like pieces of a pie, giving part of our heart to God and smaller segments to our other relationships and interests. In our human, businesslike minds we think that is equitable and fair. But God is not pleased with only a part of our heart even if he gets the biggest piece. He wants it *all,* along with *all* our soul, *all* our mind, and *all* our strength. It may seem like we'd have nothing left to share with others when we have given it all to him, but the amazing truth is when we love God completely, our hearts grow and love multiplies. We are free to love others with the most beautiful, intimate, holy affection the world has ever known — love that's *a copy* of the devotion we have for him.

God is love. When we take up permanent residence in a life of love, we live in God and God lives in us. This way, love has the run of the house, becomes at home and mature in us.
1 John 4:16–17 MSG

joy-cakes and magic teeth

Annetta E. Dellinger

*Inject a spirit of joy and optimism
into your grandchildren.
Do it by example! Begin now!*

Source unknown

It wasn't the lure of a new Easter dress made from the cloth of flowered feed bags, nor the old apple orchard with honeysuckle vines where I played hide-and-seek in the branches, nor the lush spring grass that hid the rainbow-colored Easter eggs that got me the most excited about my annual trip to Grandma's house. It was the opportunity of helping to bake a lamb-shaped cake that always kept me asking, "How many days until Easter?"

It was amazing how making the "Joy-Cakes," as Grandma called them, would somehow take all day. She told stories about our family roots while she did silly things like removing and repositioning her magical teeth. We'd laugh until our sides hurt. Secretly I'd wait for her to dust flour on my face and take lots of pictures. Even though she told me that looking that way would make the cake taste better, I knew it was really so she could say to her friends, "Look at my granddaughter!"

While I helped her mix up icing (of which there was always enough extra to lick the spoons), we sang "I Am Jesus' Little Lamb" and talked about the Good Shepherd's constant protection and everlasting love. Before I realized it, we had once again recited Psalm 23. Learning with her was such fun. I can still see the twinkle in her eye when she would say, "Ewe is loved by Jesus and me!"

When Grandma went to live with the Good Shepherd, my mother joyfully inherited the cake pans. She laughed and lovingly told me that she would carry on the tradition when she had grandchildren. And she certainly did! Hearing my children talk about their day at Grandma's house (and her magic teeth) made my heart burst with joy. I was already dreaming of the day when, hopefully, I too would have such a physical and spiritual influence as a grandmother — but without the false teeth.

Now I am once again counting days,

along with my grandchildren, until the ewes come for the bake-off. We laugh, lick, and learn — plus we've added two new traditions. First, while we are busy in the kitchen creating memories, we discuss who we should surprise with one of the cakes. We think about church shut-ins, families with little children, Sunday school teachers, and neighbors, with the list getting longer each year. After the decision is made and the cake is finished, the children carefully carry the cake to the car and hold it steady as I drive around the curves. The children try to control their nervous laughter while thinking about how surprised our recipient will be. When the lamb cake is transferred to the unsuspecting person, the joyful faces of the givers are as animated as that of the receiver.

The second tradition I've added is to talk about the reason we have Easter and God's gift of salvation. I ask my grandchildren, "If you died right now, would 'ewe' go to heaven? Why?" In fact, the grandkids now see if they can ask me before I challenge them! It's a joy to know that we will all be together with the Good Shepherd someday.

The older I get, the more I realize that my grandmother had a method to her madness, and now I'm a copycat. She took the time to prove her belief that whatever is written on the heart of a child, good or bad, will never be washed away with time. I, too, believe that each of us leaves a legacy. I caught my grandmother's love for Jesus and I pray I'm contagious with that joy too. It's the reason she called the lamb-shaped cakes "Joy-Cakes."

For we are God's workmanship, created in Christ Jesus to do good works, which God prepared in advance for us to do.
Ephesians 2:10

in the eye of
the beholder

Gracie Malone

Let me grow lovely, growing old
— so many fine things do:
Lace and ivory and gold and silks
need not be new.
There is healing in old trees,
old streets a glamour hold.
Why may not I, as well as these,
grow lovely, growing old?

Wings of Silver

My mother must have been in her late eighties when she had her picture taken for her church's pictorial directory. She had selected a lovely dress and, in my humble but biased opinion, looked absolutely *mahvelous* for a gal her age. She, on the other hand, seemed a bit disappointed with her likeness. "I guess it looks okay," she began, "but, well . . . my neck looks like an old turkey."

205

Not being one to hold back an opinion, I took one look at her sagging skin and quipped, "Mom, for an eighty-something-year-old neck, I think it looks swell." Then I tickled her under the chin and went "Gobble, gobble."

At that, Mother giggled happily. But just a few years later, a similar situation occurred. On her ninetieth birthday we celebrated on a grand scale. Her children, grandchildren, great-grandchildren, and a few great-greats gathered at First Baptist Church where she'd been a member more than sixty years. The mayor came and issued a proclamation honoring my mom as "Most Worthy Citizen" of Farmers Branch.

We took pictures — gobs of pictures, which she loved and still peruses to this day. She loved them all . . . except maybe for one. It was a warm photo that I was especially proud of because it depicted four generations from my branch of the family tree — mom, me, my daughter-in-law Jeanna, and baby Myles, just two months old. I couldn't keep from flashing the photo to anybody who would sit still long enough to take a look. Until, that is, one day when my mom put her hand on my shoulder and whispered, "I don't like that picture. Just look at my hands."

Only then did I notice the gnarled knuckles and bulging purple veins.

Looking at those hands that through the years of my life had diapered me, washed my face, wiped away tears, packed my lunch, handed over car keys, tucked an antique hanky in my pocket on the day of my wedding, and were now holding my precious grandbaby, I couldn't stop the lump rising in my throat. I choked out the words, "Those hands are beautiful to me." Mother smiled sweetly.

Later, I wondered, *when will we women give up the idea that beauty means being perfectly groomed, rail thin, and wrinkle free?* My guess is, until eternity when we will be sporting a brand-new, perfect spiritual body!

Meanwhile, as we live out our lives here on planet Earth, we need to encourage each other to take a deeper look at what's really important, to put aside our longings to present a perfect outward image and focus on things of eternal value. We could follow the example of a young deacon from my mother's church.

One Sunday morning, after a hymn, the worship leader invited the members of the congregation to greet one another. When my mom turned around and took the deacon's hand, he looked directly into her big brown eyes, saw past the crow's feet that crinkled at the corners, and got a glimpse into her soul. He uttered one word: "Beautiful!"

It's absolutely amazing what one word can do!

Even today, years after the tiny compliment was uttered, my mom loves to remind us of what that deacon said. If I could find that man today, I'd like to tell him his compliment was, well . . . absolutely *beautiful!*

And we, who with unveiled faces all reflect the Lord's glory, are being transformed into his likeness with ever-increasing glory, which comes from the Lord, who is the Spirit.
2 Corinthians 3:18

coming of age

Gracie Malone

*Family faces are magic mirrors.
Looking at people who belong to us,
we see the past, present and future.*

Gail Lumet Buckley

Now that they are widows living alone, my eighty-four-year-old mother and her slightly younger sisters, Aunt Grace and Aunt Oreta, enjoy spending an occasional weekend together. My older sister, Lois, always comes along as Mother's chauffeur, and I usually join them just in case somebody falls and can't get up. These weekends are fun for all us — three lazy days replete with stories about our kinfolk and chockfull of Texas comfort food including fried chicken, homemade pies, and sweet iced tea.

One evening, according to our usual after-dinner routine, we gathered in the living room, kicked back in five recliners, and started a conversation typical of a bunch of "Golden Girls." We began by discussing the peculiar problems of those who are, well, "chronologically gifted."

Mother said that as a person ages, her nose grows longer and her ears get bigger. I had to admit it was an anomaly I'd noticed on a few older folk. I contributed to the conversation by suggesting that such a development must be God's warning signal that the basic five senses will need some extra help in the declining years. This touched off a barrage of silly conclusions. We had all noticed how older folks get "hard of hearing," but, we wondered, do they also get "hard of smelling"? From there, the conversation moved on to the subject of hair, and we concluded that most members of the older generation lose hair up top and it sprouts in the most bizarre places. Which brings me to what has become the infamous story of my mother's aversion to such stray hairs.

One bright Saturday morning during one of the aforementioned weekend visits, we decided to go see my 103-year-old grandmother, Mama, who lived in a nursing home. I settled into the backseat of the car next to my mom as Lois and Oreta climbed up front with Aunt Grace. Bright sunshine gleamed through the rear window as we rode along. Feeling good about being the youngest member of the group, I closed my eyes, content to listen to the older women's chitchat. I opened my eyes when I heard my mom fumbling through her purse.

From the depths of her bag, Mother retrieved a shiny steel instrument and began polishing it with her hanky. I wondered what she was doing until I recognized her tweezers. Without one word of warning, my mother took aim and plucked my chin. Then she proudly displayed her prize: one curly, half-inch-long silver hair. Her mission accomplished, she replaced the tweezers in their leather case and deposited them back in her purse without missing a beat in the conversation.

As I rubbed my chin, I felt a bit perturbed at my mom for the not-so-subtle reminder that I'm aging myself. To be honest, I was not quite ready to accept senior citizen status. I felt better a few days later when I turned to the book of Psalms and read about God's faithfulness. "The Lord is faithful to all his promises and loving toward all he has made. The Lord upholds all those who fall and lifts up all who are bowed down. The eyes of all look to you, and you give them their food at the proper time. You open your hand and satisfy the desires of every living thing" (Psalm 145:13–16).

That evening, when I rested my graying head on my pillow, my fear of growing older seemed to vanish. I whispered a prayer, thanking God for three generations of women who have walked through life ahead of me, loved me well, and, in their own unique way, prepared me to face the future with confidence. What more could a woman need? Except, well . . . maybe tweezers . . . and . . . a well-lighted magnifying mirror.

*Even to your old age and gray hairs
I am he, I am he who will sustain you.
I have made you and I will carry you;
I will sustain you and I will rescue you.*
Isaiah 46:4

the white tornado

Bobbie Rill

*The foolish man seeks happiness
in the distance;
the wise grows it under his feet.*

James Oppenheim

My husband and I have been "empty nesters" for several years. But before the revolving door came to a complete stop, we realized our two children were actually going to make it. They had developed into fully functioning adults who would soon be on their own.

A strange thing happened. I began noticing a quirky smile forming on my lips and occasionally I noticed Bob suppressing the same grin. It was as though we both knew it wouldn't be long before the house would be solely ours! But shouldn't we feel sad? Was it really okay to be happy — perhaps even to celebrate? Taking the advice of friends, we headed for our favorite home-furnishings showroom with a gleam in our eyes and a spring in our step.

We had visited the store numerous times before, but this visit was different. This time we were serious shoppers. We were ready to redecorate the house from top to bottom and to replace the worn-out furniture. Entering the store, we both enthusiastically went our separate ways. Bob found a beautiful leather sofa. My head pivoted from kitchen tables, to new furniture for the patio, to glass tables, which would serve beautifully as accent pieces throughout our new home. We left feeling good that day — with no buyers' remorse.

Then Skyler Ashton Elder, affectionately known to us as the White Tornado, entered our lives! At fourteen months, with his curly blond hair and sparkling blue eyes, Skyler literally hit the floor running when our daughter, Brigette, put him down.

Since ours is not a childproof house, I followed close behind. Skyler ran into the family room as though he had mapped out his destination before his arrival. Swinging his arms, he weaved around the island that separates the family room from the kitchen, headed toward a protruding chair, then went directly to the table by the telephone.

After he cleared the table of some toys that I had strategically placed near the edge (thinking I would be way ahead of him), Skyler stretched, lifting up on one leg, and claimed a yellow highlighter near the back of the table as his special "find." While snapping the lid off and on, he moved to his next stop, the coffee table, where several *Better Homes & Gardens* and *Gourmet* magazines were displayed. He thumbed through the one on top before I was able to rescue the stack.

Next he was drawn to a plant. He stuck his little fingers into the soil and came up with a handful of dirt and pebbles. I was barely able to throw the stack of magazines down in time to stop the pebbles from entering his mouth. I brushed off his hand and headed for a cloth in the kitchen, but before I returned, Skyler had located his supply of toys stored near the entertainment center.

With books and toys now strewn all over the family room, Skyler backed up to the fireplace hearth, placed one elbow on the ledge, leaned back, and paused briefly, wondering who this crazy lady was heading toward him with a damp cloth to wash his hands and face. Sponged clean, he was off again. He had been in the house less than two minutes and already I was exhausted. Obviously, "keeping up with Skyler" was a useless endeavor, and I plopped down on the sofa.

When Skyler and his mother left that afternoon, I immediately went for the Windex, grabbed the paper towels, and headed for the coffee table. I was just about to remove the evidence of Skyler's presence when I was stopped cold in my tracks. There, on my glass table, was the complete imprint of his hands. I stepped back, staring at his handprints all over the glass table, and I couldn't bring myself to erase the impressions of my grandson's presence.

I'm discovering how to clear the path better — before Skyler's visits. But more importantly, I'm learning how to take pleasure in our time together, and I enjoy the evidence of his visits after he leaves. The door of my heart and my home will always be open to that child. And I wouldn't trade those tiny fingerprints all over my house for anything in the world!

My little "white tornado" reminds me that even when I mess things up, my heavenly Father loves me and enjoys my presence.

*I have loved you
with an everlasting love;
I have drawn you with loving-kindness.*
Jeremiah 31:3

fit for a queen

Gracie Malone

*Brain cells come and brain cells go,
but fat cells live forever.*

Anonymous

As the story goes, a rather large woman was lumbering down the aisle in the grocery store picking up items along the way. Her preschool grandson was tagging along, asking questions about every item she selected.

She paused at the panty hose display, made her choice, and tossed the package into the cart. The egg-shaped design of the package must have piqued the youngster's curiosity, for the little guy almost tipped the cart over as he climbed on the front and retrieved the package from the bottom of the basket. He clutched the item in his tiny extended hand and, in a booming tone, sounded out the words on the label: "Queen size!"

As several nearby shoppers turned to look, the red-faced grandma grabbed the item from the child's hand, but not before he shouted, "Grandma, are these the same size as our mattress?"

When I heard this tale, I couldn't hold back a wicked giggle. That poor grandma must have been soooo embarrassed! But I giggled for another reason as well. For I can identify with this young man's confusion. How can something "queen size" be squeezed into a package no bigger than an egg? Furthermore, why is it when a pair of "queen-size" hose is removed from the package and completely unfurled, it seems more "fit" for Tinker Bell than a queen?

As I thought about this story, I remembered facing my own battle with a pair of panty hose one Sunday morning as I was getting ready for church. I had carefully opened a package of so-called "Queen Size" hosiery and shook out the wrinkles. As I examined the eight-inch waistband trying to locate the back, the tiny undergarment's twelve-inch-long legs floated on the air like a pair of butterfly wings. I couldn't help but wonder about the elasticity of the nylon fibers as I held the garment up to the light. It was then that I noticed my hubby watching me. He took one look at the minuscule pair of panty hose, patted me on my . . . well . . . rather *ample* backside, and with great conviction in his voice proclaimed, "I believe in miracles!"

Sure enough, I was able to pull on those panty hose and still manage to walk. In fact, I not only wore them to church but also to the drugstore the next day when I went shopping with my six-year-old granddaughter, Mary Catherine.

The little girl stood close beside me as I examined a line of cosmetics, trying to find just the right moisturizer. (Decisions, decisions!) Mary, truly a girly-girl who loves to play with makeup, seemed caught up in the process. After a few minutes she selected a well-advertised brand of cream and, in a loud tone, suggested, "Grandma Gracie, here! Try this Oil-of-Ole-Lady."

Sometimes I think God gives us grandchildren to keep us humble. For we can always count on them to give an opinion based upon the unabashed, unadulterated truth. But even though they see us just as we are, our precious grandkids really don't care if we're fat or thin, tall or short, drop-dead gorgeous, or slightly wrinkled and gray. They love us unconditionally with the most amazing selfless love we'll ever experience this side of heaven.

Is there a grandma among us who couldn't use a liberal dose of that kind of devotion? Seems to me that's love fit for a queen.

If we love one another, God dwells deeply within us, and his love becomes complete in us — perfect love!
1 John 4:12 MSG

tuesdays with granny

Deborah P. Brunt

When we do the best that we can,
we never know what miracle
is wrought in our life,
or in the life of another.

Helen Keller

Every other Tuesday, my girls and I visited her. We opened the back door of Whitfield Nursing Home, strode down the long hall, turned right at the nurses' station and stepped into her room. I'd say, "Hello, Granny! It's Deborah, Megan, and Amanda. How are you doing today?"

Sometimes my paternal grandmother sat looking at us without giving a clue as to whether she knew who we were. More often, she smiled. On a really good day, she answered, "Not doing well" or "I'm better."

The girls and I would perch on Granny's

bed, next to the chair where she sat, and tell her all the family news we knew. Megan and Amanda, then six and four, would replace the two drawings that hung on Granny's closet door with two new drawings they'd brought.

Then we sang for her. Of course, Megan and Amanda chose the songs. Our repertoire included "Jesus Loves Me," "Climb, Climb Up Sunshine Mountain," "She'll Be Comin' Around the Mountain," and a number of other children's choruses and nursery songs.

Typically, the girls stood, using the metal rods at the bed's corners as microphones. They often did silly stunts while singing. Sometimes Granny would shake her head and say, "Look at that." Or she might look past us into another world she was already seeing. If the girls noticed that they weren't being noticed, they acted even sillier.

Settling them down a bit, I'd ask Megan to read aloud a story or two from her first-grade reader. Then the girls would take turns "reading" or saying Bible verses, and I'd read a short Scripture passage. One week, I read from Psalm 71:5: "For you have been my hope, O Sovereign Lord, my confidence since my youth . . . Do not cast me away when I am old; do not forsake me when my strength is gone."

Sometimes Granny would try to tell us something. I could see the frustration in her eyes when the words got all jumbled coming out of her mouth. One week, she surprised us all. Looking directly at me, she said, "You've been so good to me."

About forty-five minutes after we arrived, I'd say a short prayer for Granny. Then we took turns kissing her. Even if she paid little attention during the rest of our visit, she would break into a big smile as each of the girls kissed her.

We'd leave. Once out the door, I'd take one last look back and see her sitting quietly in her chair, looking at the wall. She spent almost all her waking hours sitting like that. A disease that destroys brain cells had robbed her of the ability to think clearly, to say more than three words, to eat solid foods, or to walk. On the way home, the girls would sometimes ask, "Mama, why are you crying?"

One wintry Sunday morning not long after Valentine's Day, my mother called me out of church to tell me Granny had collapsed in her room at the nursing home. She died before I could reach the hospital.

That Sunday, Megan and Amanda cried for a great-grandmother who had never taken them anywhere or bought them anything, who had not spoken more than five full sentences to them in their whole lives.

Two handmade valentines decorated Granny's closet door for more than a week before her death. The large red hearts glued onto white construction paper hung so she could see them from her bed. Each card declared, "I love you."

Even if Granny couldn't read the words anymore, I believe she understood them. She knew we meant them.

And maybe, just maybe, our visits helped her understand something else. Maybe as we spoke and sang and acted silly, she heard the voice of the God she trusted, saying, "I love you."

You see, we went for forty-five minutes every other week, but he never left.*

For you have been my hope,
O Sovereign Lord,
my confidence since my youth.
Do not cast me away when I am old;
do not forsake me when my strength
is gone.
Psalm 71:5, 9

* Adapted from a piece that was included as part of a longer article in *Moody Magazine*, June 1993.

About Carol Kent, General Editor

Carol Kent is a popular international public speaker best known for being dynamic, humorous, encouraging, and biblical. She is a former radio show cohost and has been a guest on numerous television and radio programs. She is the president of Speak Up Speaker Services, a Christian speakers' bureau, and the founder and director of Speak Up With Confidence seminars, a ministry committed to helping Christians develop their communication skills. She has also founded the nonprofit organization Speak Up for Hope, which benefits the families of incarcerated individuals. A member of the National Speakers Association, Carol is often scheduled more than a year in advance for keynote addresses at conferences and retreats throughout the United States and abroad.

She holds a master's degree in communication arts and a bachelor's degree in speech education. Her books include:

When I Lay My Isaac Down, *Becoming a Woman of Influence*, *Mothers Have Angel Wings*, *Secret Longings of the Heart*, *Tame Your Fears*, *Speak Up With Confidence*, and *Detours, Tow Trucks, and Angels in Disguise*. She has also cowritten with Karen Lee-Thorp *My Soul's Journey* and the *Designed for Influence* Bible Studies. Carol has been featured on the cover of *Today's Christian Woman* and her articles have been published in a wide variety of magazines. To schedule Carol to speak for your event, call 888-870-7719 or contact her at *www.SpeakUpSpeakerServices.com* or *www.CarolKent.org*.

About Gracie Malone

It wasn't until after their youngest son headed off to college that Gracie mailed an article she'd written to a magazine. She wondered if, just maybe, they'd be interested in publishing it. They were! (There is life after kids.) Her first article came out in *Moody Magazine* in 1994. Since then, Gracie's work has been published several times in *Moody* and in other well-known magazines including *Discipleship Journal*, *Decision*, *Women Alive*, *Christian Parenting Today*, *Home Life*, *Celebrate Life*, and *The Virtuous Woman*.

Gracie's latest works include *Off My Rocker — Grandparenting Ain't What It Used to Be* and *Still Making Waves — Creating a Splash in Midlife and Beyond*. *Courage for the Chicken-Hearted*, Gracie's first book project, coauthored with four friends affectionately dubbed "Hens with Pens," quickly became a bestseller. The success of her first book encouraged its sequel the next year, *Eggstra Courage for the Chicken-Hearted*. Gracie has contributed to several other books, including *It Took This Long to Learn This Much, Humor for a Mom's Heart, Humor for a Woman's Heart*, and the Women of Faith compilation *She Who Laughs, Lasts*.

In addition to writing, Gracie is a Bible study teacher, Precept Leader, and much-loved speaker for women's conferences and retreats. Gracie and her husband Joe live in Grapevine, Texas, near their children and grandchildren.

To schedule Gracie to speak for your event, call 888-870-7719, or request promotional material through *www.SpeakUp SpeakerServices.com*. You can contact Gracie online at *www.graciemalone.com*, by email at gracie@graciemalone.com, or by phone/fax at 817-488-2317.

Contributors

Deborah P. Brunt writes a weekly column that appears in several newspapers, on numerous websites, and is distributed by email. She has written three books and contributed to several others. She is a women's missions and ministries specialist for Oklahoma Baptists. To receive Deborah's weekly columns by email, or for scheduling information, contact her at dbrunt@bgco.org or call 405-942-3800.

Annetta E. Dellinger is known as "The Joy Lady." She is founder and president of Joyful Ministries and a speaker with Speak Up Speaker Services. She is author of thirty books, including *Be Joyful . . . Who Me? Mini Joy-Spirations to Energize Your Day*. For information, contact Annetta at *www.Annettadellinger.com*. To schedule Annetta for a speaking engagement, call 888-870-7719.

Jennie Afman Dimkoff is the president of Storyline Ministries Inc. and is the author of *Night Whispers: Bedtime Bible Stories for Women* and *More Night Whispers: Bedtime Bible Stories for Women*. She is also is a speaker/trainer with Speak Up With Confidence seminars. For additional information, please visit her website at *www.Jennie AfmanDimkoff.com*. To schedule Jennie as a speaker for your next event, call 888-870-7719.

Bonnie Afman Emmorey is a speaker consultant with Speak Up Speaker Services and teaches communications skills for Speak Up With Confidence seminars and is helping launch Speak Up for Hope. For additional information, go to *www.SpeakUp SpeakerServices.com* and *www.SpeakUp ForHope.com*.

Judy Hampton is an international keynote speaker for women's conferences and the author of the book *Under the Circumstances*. For additional information, visit her website at *www.judyhampton.com*. To schedule Judy for your next event, call 888-870-7719.

Phyllis Olay Harmony is the president of Speaking in Harmony. She travels nationally as a keynote speaker, retreat leader, and workshop presenter. For additional information, visit her website at *www.speakinginharmony.com.*

Cynthia Spell Humbert was a Christian counselor at the Minirth-Meier Clinic in Dallas, Texas, for seven years. She is the author of *Deceived by Shame, Desired by God.* Cynthia travels nationally as a keynote speaker for women's conferences and marriage retreats. To schedule Cynthia as a speaker for your next event, call 888-870-7719.

Ginger Kamps is the director of Marketplace Missionary Ministry through City LinC Ministries in Battle Creek, Michigan. One of her passions in life is to open the eyes of Christ-followers to see the mission field in their spheres of influence and to advance his kingdom in the marketplace. You may contact her at gingerkamps@citylinc.org.

Laura Leathers writes articles for several magazines, including *Just Between Us, The Proverbs 31 Newsletter*, and *Tea Room Guide & Digest*. She also writes and edits her own quarterly newsletter, *Teacups and Friends*. She is a Bible study leader, a mentor, and a speaker for churches, conferences, and retreats. To contact Laura for your next event, go to *www.LauraLeathers.com*.

Heidi McLaughlin is a retreat and seminar speaker who shares motivational and encouraging ideas with women of all ages. For more information call 250-707-0924 or email Heidi at angelscorner@shaw.ca.

Shari Minke often portrays humorous characters, such as "Norma Lee Crotchety," a feisty, eighty-year-old preacher's wife; "Selma Kidds," a pregnant mom expecting her fourteenth child; and "Liza Little," a precocious five-year-old. Her biblical presentations and inspirational speaking will move you as much as her humor will delight you. Shari Minke can be contacted at 23870 Greening Dr., Novi, MI 48375, or by phone at 248-348-5212.

Linda Neff is the author of *Love, Laughter, and Tears — Poems for All of Life*. She works as a facilitator for Speak Up With Confidence seminars and teaches high school English in Guelph, Ontario, Canada.

Diana Pintar is the president of the Next Step Ministries Inc. and travels nationally as a speaker for women's conferences and retreats. Diana is a speaker/trainer with Speak Up With Confidence seminars. For additional information, visit her website at *www.TheNextStepOnline.com*. To schedule Diana as a speaker for your next event, call 888-870-7719.

Bobbie Rill is the director of Women of Virtue, a national conference and radio ministry. Bobbie is a frequent speaker for women's events, and she helps women reach their potential through her private counseling practice, training seminars, and personal coaching. To schedule Bobbie for your next women's event, call 888-870-7719, or for information regarding her training and coaching services, call 520-904-2804.

Ginger Shaw is a communications trainer for Speak Up With Confidence seminars. She is a playwright and an actress who has frequently appeared on *Turning Point* with Dr. David Jeremiah. For information on scheduling Ginger to speak at your next leadership training seminar or women's conference, call 888-870-7719.

Debi Stack is a speaker to women's groups and radio audiences on the topics of stress, perfectionism, and over-commitment, and author of *Martha to the Max: Balanced Living for Perfectionists*. For additional information, visit her website at *www.maxedout.net*. To schedule Debi as a speaker for your event, call 800-433-6633.

Vicki Tiede is a wife, mother, teacher, and motivational speaker. For additional information, visit her website at *www.Grace Lessons.com*. To schedule Vicki as a speaker, contact her at Vicki@GraceLessons.com or by phone at 507-254-5656.

Lynn Warren is a contributing writer at *Homebodies* (*www.homebodies.org*), a support website for present and prospective stay-at-home moms.

Jeanne Zornes is a women's retreat and conference speaker and a writer of hundreds of articles and seven books, including *When I Prayed for Patience . . . God Let Me Have It!* She lives in Washington State. Contact her at P.O. Box 4362, Wenatchee, WA 98807-4392.

MARTIN HILL

EARTH TO EARTH

ART INSPIRED BY NATURE'S DESIGN

FOREWORD SIR EDMUND HILLARY

INTRODUCTION JONATHON PORRITT

I WORK IN NATURE

BECAUSE WE ARE NATURE.

FOREWORD

Martin Hill has climbed in many parts of the world and, like myself and most other climbers, has witnessed the many changes that have occurred in the wilderness and nature.

No one who has any feeling for the beauty of nature or any concern for humankind could be unmoved by the problems faced by our natural environment. Change for the better is inevitably slow, but change and improvement we are certainly seeing.

An increasingly large number of people around the world are using their skills to bring the environment's problems to the world's attention. Thankfully, a sense of environmental responsibility is gradually being adopted by an ever wider audience.

Martin Hill creates and publishes environmental artworks that reveal his love for the earth's environment and his desire to protect it. Recognizing current lifestyles are unsustainable, he works to inspire sustainable ethical design to bring us into balance with the natural world upon which we rely.

The world is still very beautiful; every effort must be made to preserve it. I admire Martin's unique way of showing us the beauty of nature, not only visually, but metaphorically, because the cyclical way in which nature works is a guide to our own destiny, should we choose to see it.

The responsible modern adventurer is one who not only explores, but protects as well. I congratulate Martin Hill for his vision and perseverance in creating the powerful works in this book. I hope you will see in them the essence of the artist's philosophy.

SIR EDMUND HILLARY

INTRODUCTION

As we slowly stir ourselves into deeper awareness of our environmental predicament, the question I get asked most often these days is a simple one: "Do we still have time?"—time to turn around this terminally destructive model of economic progress and develop instead an elegant and equitable way of living sustainably on Planet Earth.

At one level, the answer has to be one of those proverbial no-brainers. Given that we don't actually have a choice about learning to live sustainably on Planet Earth (inasmuch as if we don't, we will have simply engineered our own extinction!), the answer must be "yes." "But at what cost?" is a far trickier inquiry.

There are many who now believe that it is already too late to achieve this necessary transition in a planned and precautionary way. Climate scientists are now focused on the threat of what is described as "dangerous climate change"—that point at which the atmosphere warms up so fast (as a consequence of all the CO_2 and other greenhouse gases we're putting into it) that we can no longer control the consequences. And the evidence available to us from ice cores going back hundreds of thousands of years is indeed pretty gloomy on that score: beyond a certain point, the gradual buildup of greenhouse gases in the atmosphere does not lead to a gradual warming, but to dramatic, nonlinear shifts from one climate state to another.

To point out to people, in that emerging context, that we only have a few years to avoid the scariest of all tipping points (the point at which we lose the ability to control our own destiny on Planet Earth) is a necessary part of challenging deep-rooted patterns of denial in society today. But this is a difficult balancing act: all too often, fear begets only paralysis rather than the kind of purposeful commitment to action and changed behavior that is now so desperately needed.

After more than thirty years trying to bring home to people the sheer impossibility of our current model of progress, my obsession with overcoming today's systematized patterns of denial is now overwhelming. During that time, the science underpinning this particular critique of progress has become stronger and stronger by the year. Even the economics are beginning to come together, with the recent report on the economics of climate change from Sir Nicholas Stern demonstrating that it will cost between five and twenty times more to do nothing about climate change than it will to get it sorted. As he says, "The world does not need to choose between averting climate change and promoting growth and development."

But still nothing happens—or nothing much, to be more accurate. Which leads me to ask what else has to be done if the combined weight of overwhelming scientific evidence and an impeccable economic rationale has about as much impact as a bishop's sermon in a late-night casino?

Perhaps we aren't experiencing as yet the real pain of the loss to come—with not enough "pre-traumatic stress disorder" to shake us all out of our inertia, to help us feel our way through to a different model of progress in which we seek to cohabit with rather than subjugate the natural world. Martin Hill's life's work has been about opening people's eyes to see the natural world differently, to really see that world (and our part in it) rather than pass on by as so many semidetached tourists staring vacantly through the windows of their luxury coach. Substitute the insights of empathy-driven relationship for the depersonalized metrics of scientific rationalism and cost-benefit analysis, and a different truth begins to emerge.

Unless we're lucky enough to have regular, generous contact with the natural world for ourselves, we can't help but see that world in large part through the eyes of others. Our need for mentors and interpreters has never been greater—not just to reawaken our sense of wonder, but to be stimulated to think much more deeply about our relationship with the natural world. Wonder without relationship is little more than voyeurism. Indeed, some of the harsher critics of the output of the BBC's

Natural History Unit have sometimes accused producers (and even David Attenborough himself) of peddling an upmarket form of "nature pornography."

Personally, I think this is unfair. At the heart of the concept of sustainability lies an often unspoken philosophical challenge: to rediscover the reality of interdependence. Having spent several centuries promoting a model of progress that emphasizes our independence of and separation from the rest of the natural world, we now know how foolish and arrogant that has been. Every wound inflicted on the earth is a self-inflicted wound on us as well. The American philosopher Willis Harman identified "the ontological assumption of separateness" as the single most lethal illusion that has undermined our model of progress since the start of the Industrial Revolution.

Relearning that state of total dependency is the first step on the way to "learning to live by nature's design"—one of the most compelling challenges that Martin's wonderfully inspiring book offers us here. Without that kind of new intelligence, the living, breathing intelligence that flows from being re-embedded in the natural world, it will be hard if not impossible to transform today's dominant mindsets—and lifestyles and behavior won't change until those mindsets change first.

This inevitably sounds like a long and winding road, and no more guaranteed to deliver a sustainable outcome than the scientific and economic rationalism on which we depend so heavily today. But it is a road that we now have to navigate in double-quick time, and with joy in our hearts in the presence of nature rather than today's hemlock of despair creeping slowly through our hearts and minds.

JONATHON PORRITT, FOUNDER-DIRECTOR, FORUM FOR THE FUTURE; CHAIRMAN, U.K. SUSTAINABLE DEVELOPMENT COMMISSION

MY INSPIRATION COMES
FROM BEING IMMERSED
IN AND LEARNING FROM
THE NATURAL WORLD.

MY MATERIALS COME
FROM THE EARTH TO
WHICH THEY RETURN
HARMLESSLY AFTER USE.

MY PHOTOGRAPHS ARE
MADE WITH THE SAME
SUNLIGHT THAT POWERS
ALL THE EARTH'S LIVING
SYSTEMS.

MY SCULPTURES ARE
A RESPONSE TO THE
FUNDAMENTAL CONFLICT
BETWEEN THE
DESTRUCTIVE LINEAR
DESIGN OF HUMAN
ECONOMIC SYSTEMS
AND NATURE'S EVOLVED
CYCLICAL DESIGN.

LEARNING TO LIVE BY NATURE'S DESIGN IS OUR ONLY HOPE FOR THE FUTURE.

THE STARTING POINT: RESPECT NATURE.

THE ENDING POINT: IMITATE NATURE.

GUNTER PAULI, founder of ZERO EMISSIONS RESEARCH INITIATIVE (ZERI)

Our human destiny is inextricably
linked to the actions of all living things.
Respecting this principle is the
fundamental challenge in changing
the nature of business.

PAUL HAWKEN, environmentalist

The choice before us is urgent and
important: it can neither be postponed
nor ignored. The choice: evolution
or extinction.

ERVIN LÁSZLÓ, scientific philosopher

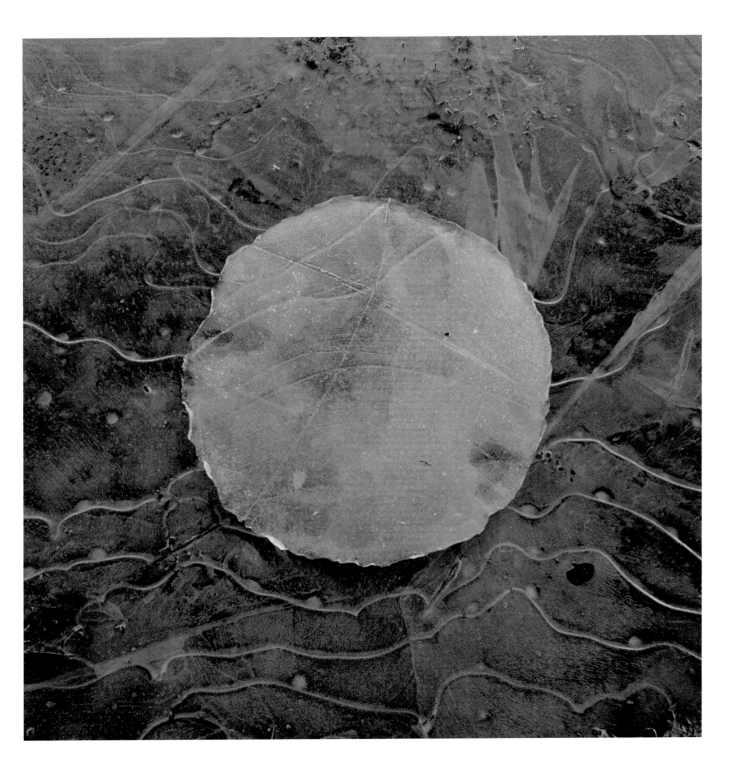

Unless we change direction, we are likely
to end up where we are going.

CHINESE PROVERB

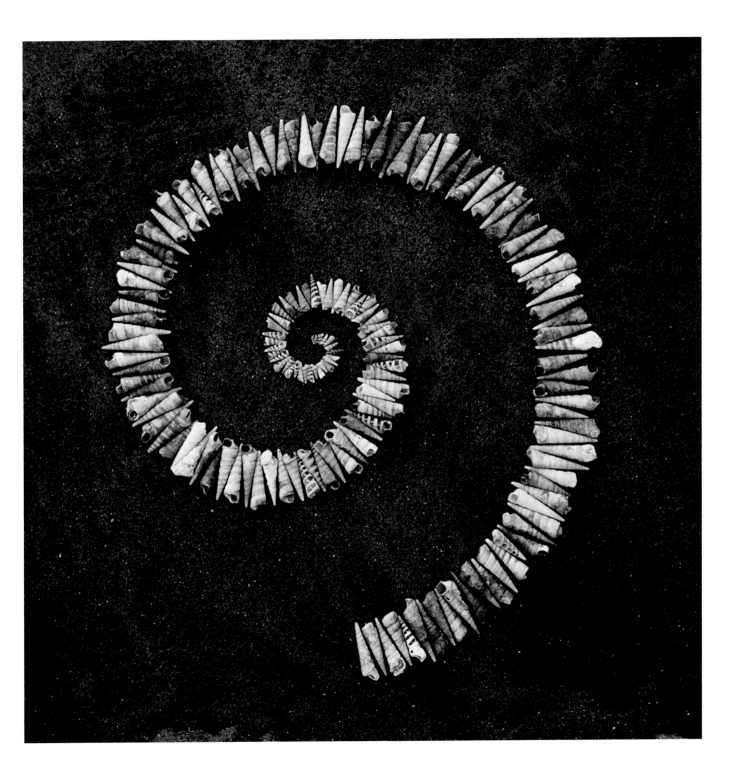

If people are to prosper within the natural world, all the products and materials manufactured by industry must after each useful life provide nourishment for something new.

WILLIAM McDONOUGH, architect

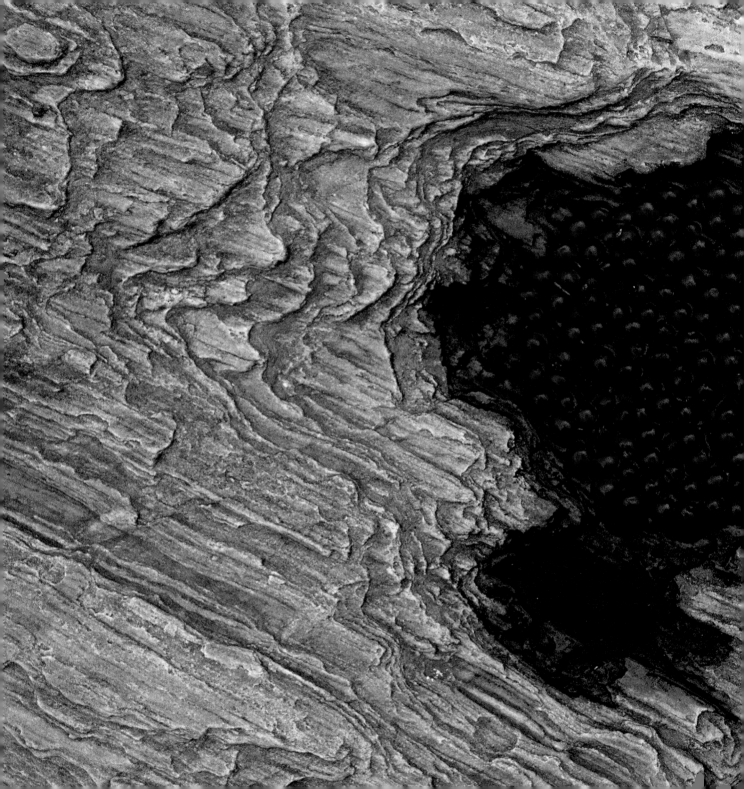

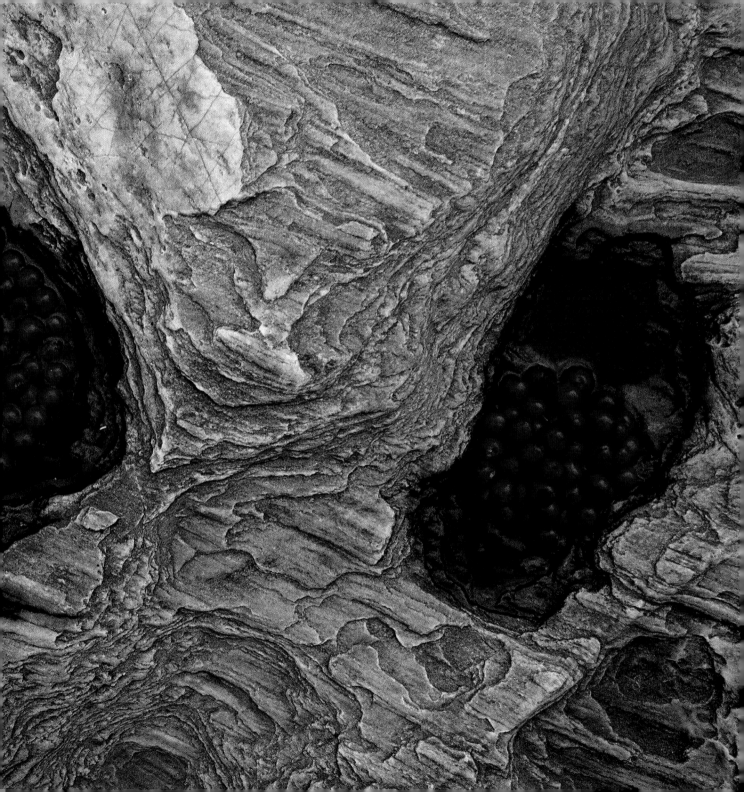

EACH DAY MORE SOLAR ENERGY FALLS TO THE EARTH THAN THE TOTAL AMOUNT OF ENERGY THE PLANET'S SIX BILLION INHABITANTS WOULD CONSUME IN TWENTY-FIVE YEARS.

The only processes we can rely
on indefinitely are cyclical; all linear
processes must eventually come to
an end.

DR. KARL-HENRIK ROBÉRT,
founder of THE NATURAL STEP

The smallest deed is better than the greatest intention.

JOHN BURROUGHS, naturalist and essayist

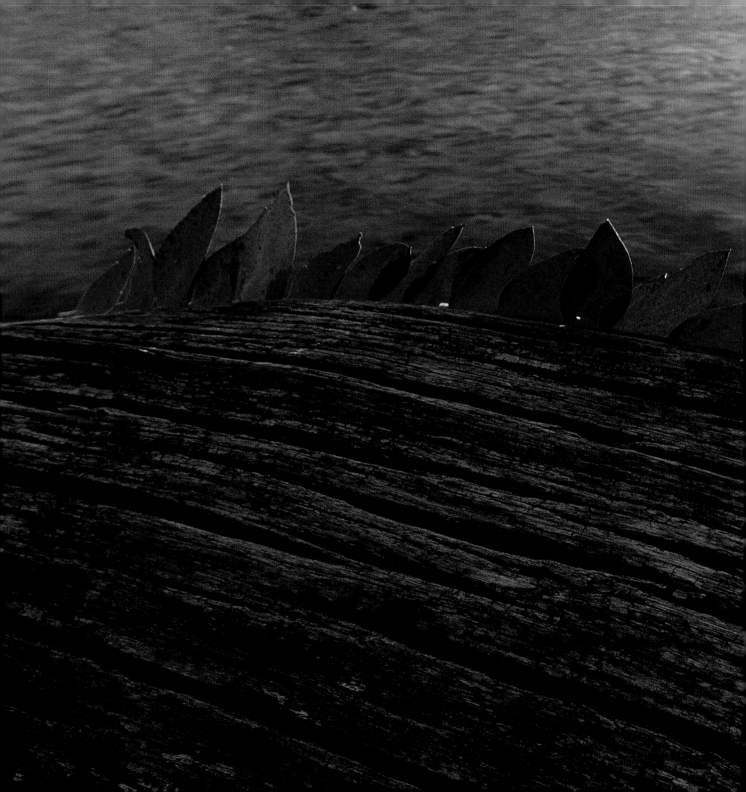

It is not enough to be friendly toward the environment—we must adapt to it.

ANDERS C. MOBERG, former president of IKEA

It is difficult to get a man to understand
something when his salary depends on
not understanding it.

From the documentary
AN INCONVENIENT TRUTH, presented
by Al Gore

FOR ALL AT LAST RETURNS TO
THE SEA—TO OCEANUS, THE
OCEAN RIVER, LIKE THE EVER
FLOWING STREAM OF TIME,
THE BEGINNING AND THE END.

We are surrounded by information and information technology. But they do not tell us what we need to know: how to live in balance with the natural systems of the planet.

DR. DAVID SUZUKI, scientist and environmentalist

The midcourse correction I think earth
and humanity need probably depends on,
more than any other thing, changed minds,
i.e. new paradigms.

RAY ANDERSON, founder and chairman
of INTERFACE, INC.

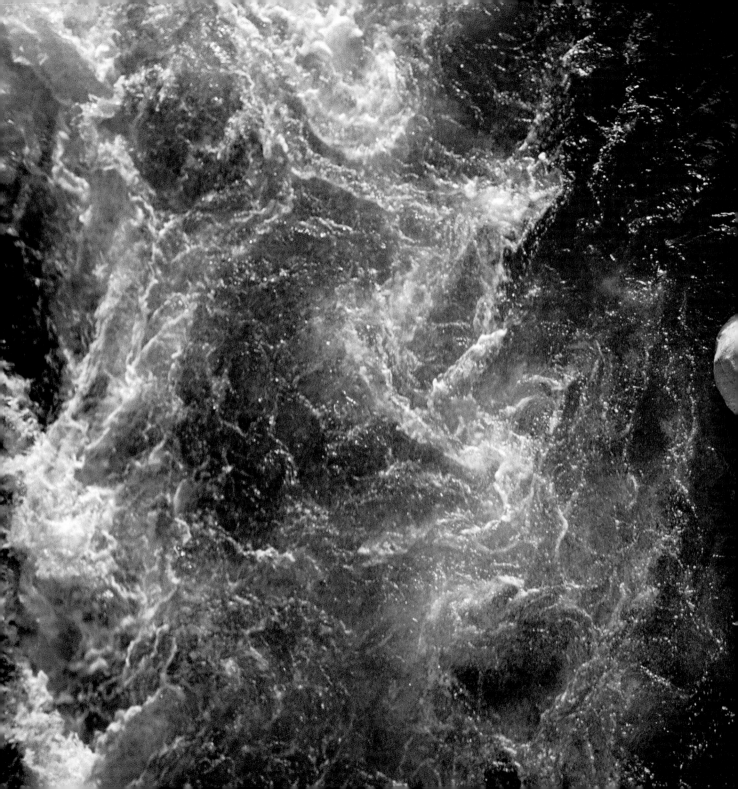

We cannot continue to take our wealth
from nature. We must learn a new way,
a way to cultivate wealth like nature, to
provide affluence without effluence.

TACHI KIUCHI, chairman of FUTURE
500

Designers should define their role broadly
as agents of good in the world, and limit
their work to "legitimate" products: those that
are needed, and those that can be made
without damage to nature or—through the
unethical actions of manufacturers
and investors—damage to people.

PHILIPPE STARCK, designer

Hydrocarbons? No, thanks.
Carbohydrates? Yes, please.

EDWIN DATSCHEFSKI, biothinker

WHAT USE IS A HOUSE IF YOU HAVEN'T GOT A TOLERABLE PLANET TO PUT IT ON?

HENRY DAVID THOREAU, author

If one desires a change, one must
be that change before that change
can take place.

GITA BELLIN, author

A thing is right when it tends to preserve the integrity, stability, and beauty of the biotic community. It is wrong when it tends otherwise.

ALDO LEOPOLD, conservationist

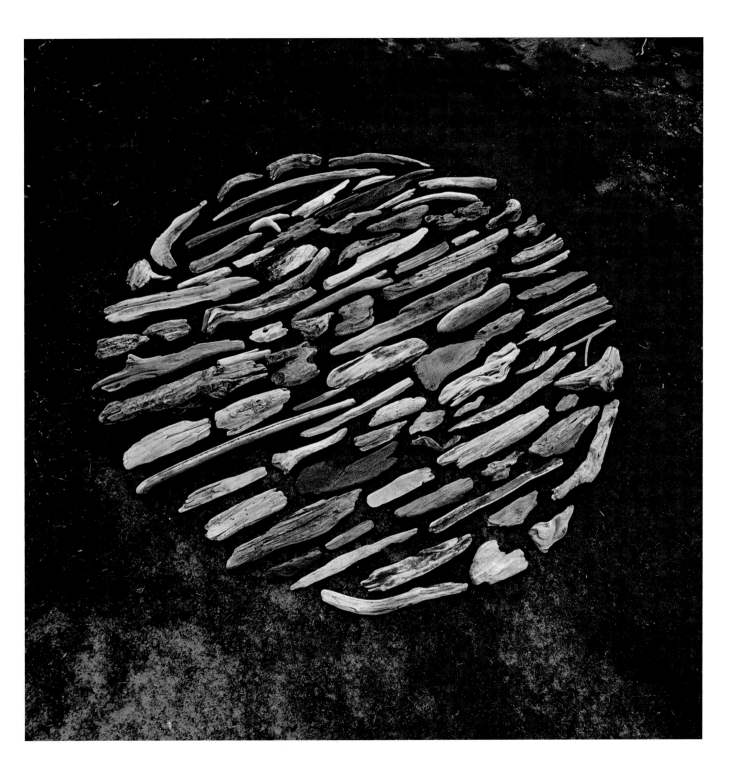

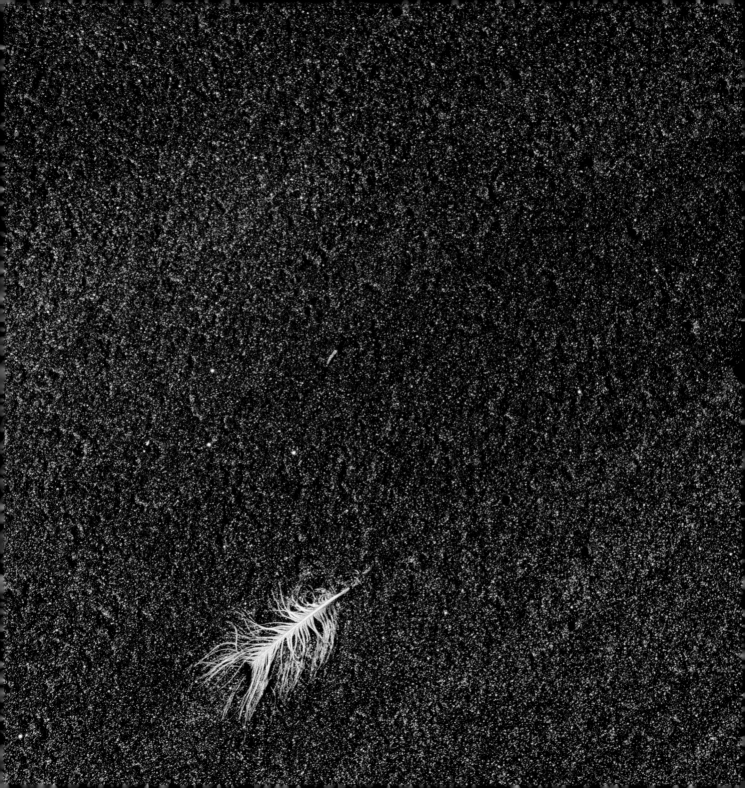

THERE IS NO NEED TO INVENT
A SUSTAINABLE WORLD;
THAT'S BEEN DONE ALREADY.
IT'S ALL AROUND US.

JANINE M. BENYUS, biologist

Embrace the arrangements that have shaken down in the evolutionary process and try to mimic them, ever mindful that human cleverness must remain subordinate to nature's wisdom.

WES JACKSON, agriculturalist and founder of THE U.S. LAND INSTITUTE

Man is the only species capable of
generating waste—things that no other
life on earth wants to have.

GUNTER PAULI, founder of
ZERO EMISSIONS RESEARCH
INITIATIVE (ZERI)

The twentieth century will be chiefly
remembered by future generations not
as an era of political conflicts or technical
innovations, but as an age in which
human society dared to think of the
welfare of the whole human race as a
practical objective.

ARNOLD J. TOYNBEE, historian

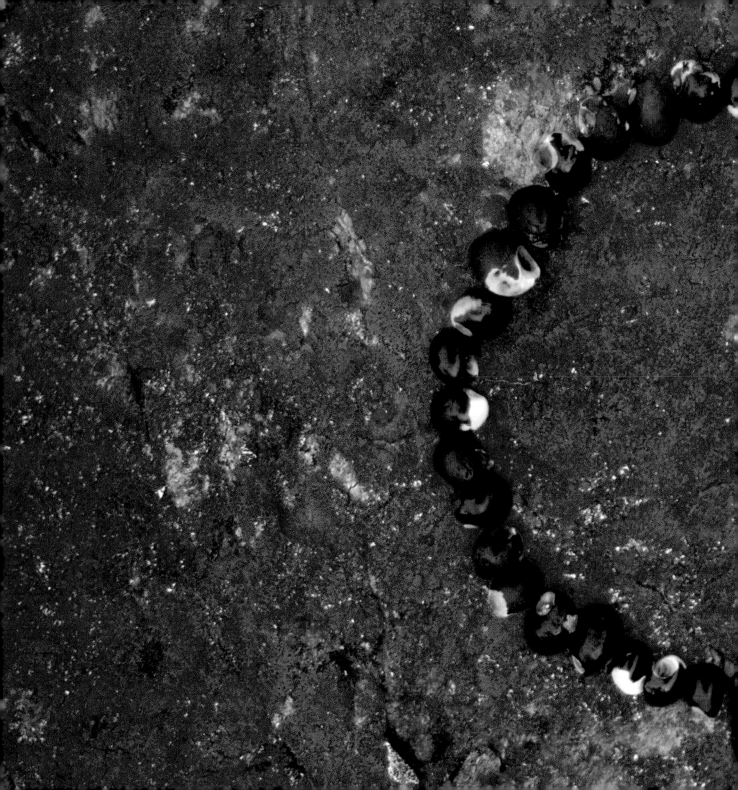

The water that we have now is the same water that we have always had on this planet. There is no new water.

DR. KARL-HENRIK ROBÈRT, founder of THE NATURAL STEP

What is remarkable about this period
in history is the degree of agreement
that is forming globally about the
relationship between human and
living systems.

PAUL HAWKEN, environmentalist

THE TASK IS NOT SO MUCH TO SEE WHAT NO ONE HAS SEEN, BUT TO THINK WHAT NO ONE HAS THOUGHT ABOUT THAT WHICH EVERYONE SEES.

ARTHUR SCHOPENHAUER, philosopher and author

Things are either devolving toward
or evolving from nothingness.

LEONARD KOREN, author

In the long term, the economy and the environment are the same thing. If it's unenvironmental it is uneconomical. That is the rule of nature.

MOLLIE BEATTIE, former director of the U.S. FISH AND WILDLIFE SERVICE

The more clearly we can focus our
attention on the wonders and realities of
the universe, the less taste we shall have
for destruction.

RACHEL CARSON, Author and
environmentalist

The wilderness holds answers to more
questions than we have yet learned to ask.

NANCY NEWHALL, photographer and
conservationist

Earth and sky, woods and fields, lakes
and rivers, the mountain and the sea,
are excellent schoolmasters and teach
some of us more than we can ever learn
from books.

SIR JOHN LUBBOCK, politician and
biologist

JOY IN LOOKING AND
COMPREHENDING
IS NATURE'S MOST
BEAUTIFUL GIFT.

ALBERT EINSTEIN, physicist

Technological progress has merely
provided us more efficient means for
going backward.

ALDOUS HUXLEY, author

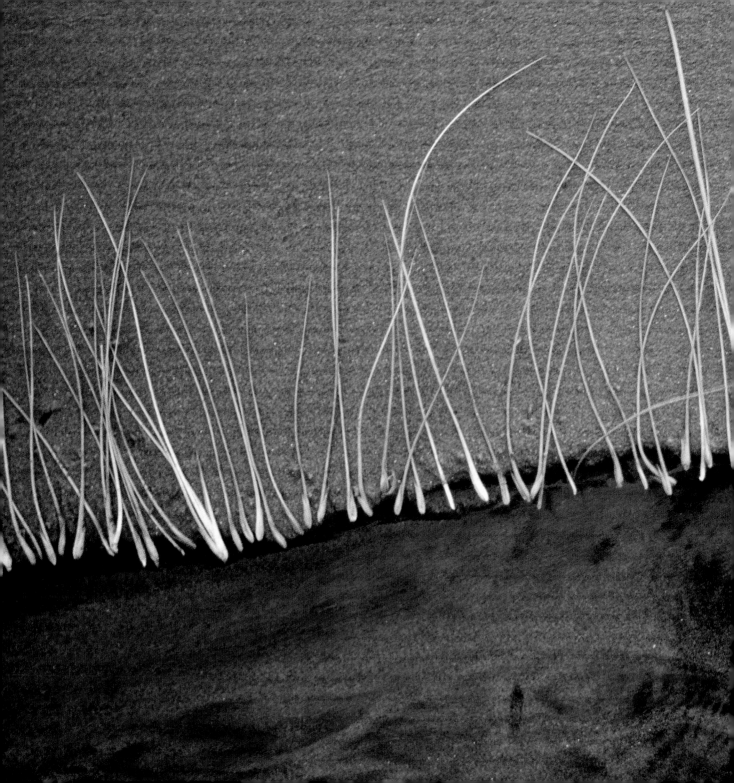

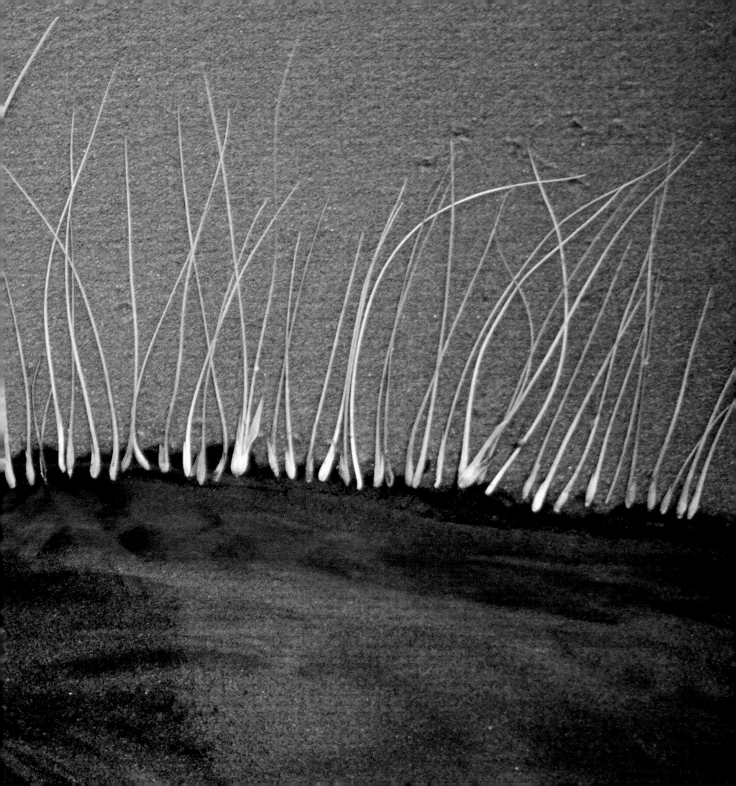

Study nature, love nature, stay close to
nature. It will never fail you.

ANONYMOUS

The most powerful survival principle of life is diversity; there is no single right way that works—there will be hundreds of thousands.

DR. DAVID SUZUKI, scientist and environmentalist

We do not inherit the earth from our
ancestors; we borrow it from our children.

NATIVE AMERICAN PROVERB

The future will be green or not at all. This truth lies at the heart of humankind's most pressing challenge: to learn to live in harmony with the earth on a genuinely sustainable basis.

JONATHON PORRITT, founder-director, FORUM FOR THE FUTURE; chairman, U.K. SUSTAINABLE DEVELOPMENT COMMISSION

The veneration of progress for its own
sake has resulted in a world where
things take precedence over people.

PHILIPPE STARCK, designer

PROFESSOR KARL-HENRIK ROBÈRT, M.D., PH.D., FOUNDER OF THE NATURAL STEP

DR. KARL-HENRIK ROBÈRT IS ONE OF SWEDEN'S FOREMOST CANCER SCIENTISTS WHO, IN 1989, INITIATED AN ENVIRONMENTAL MOVEMENT CALLED "THE NATURAL STEP," WHICH PROVIDED SYSTEM CONDITIONS FOR SOCIAL AND ECOLOGICAL SUSTAINABILITY. TOGETHER WITH A GROWING NETWORK OF SCIENTISTS AND DECISION MAKERS IN BUSINESS AND POLITICS, THESE CONDITIONS HAVE BEEN ELABORATED INTO A CONCRETE FRAMEWORK FOR STRATEGIC PLANNING TOWARD SUSTAINABILITY.

KARL-HENRIK HAS WRITTEN MANY BOOKS AND OTHER PUBLICATIONS ON SUSTAINABILITY, PROMOTING AWARENESS OF THE LINK BETWEEN ECOLOGY, ECONOMY, AND TECHNOLOGY. IN 1999 HE WAS AWARDED THE GREEN CROSS AWARD FOR INTERNATIONAL LEADERSHIP, AND IN 2000 HE WON THE BLUE PLANET PRIZE.

Art in nature is all about the connectedness between people, and between people and nature.

Regardless of where the primary focus of interest is placed in the sustainability debate—social or ecological—the fact remains that human behavior is the key to leveraging change. Therefore we must focus on people and society.

The social tissue of the global human society is currently suffering from many impacts, and perhaps the worst of these is the gradual loss of meaningful stories. This is a global disease and leads to a shrinking of perspective. Instead of forming worthwhile goals we concentrate on results; instead of seeing the whole picture we recognize only the details; instead of valuing community we care only about ourselves.

This social disease can only be cured by meaningful stories—the stories that provide the cultural glue between people. It is true that the reason for needing nature, and each other, can be explained and verified in scientific terms, but people are a social species.

It is our stories—or myths—that tell us about connectedness and why we need nature and each other. However, the full meaning of that connectedness also requires us to use another dimension of our mental capacity—one that goes beyond intellectual understanding and into the realm of art. It's like seeing in the dark: you can see things more clearly if you look indirectly at them instead of focusing directly on them.

Martin Hill's art allows us to fully understand the meaning of connectedness. His work tells us these stories—and his inspiration comes from learning from nature's design.

Karl-Henrik Robèrt

RAY C. ANDERSON,
FOUNDER AND CHAIRMAN OF INTERFACE, INC.

AFTER GRADUATING FROM THE GEORGIA INSTITUTE OF TECHNOLOGY AS AN INDUSTRIAL ENGINEER, RAY ANDERSON APPLIED HIS ENTREPRENEURIAL SPIRIT TO BUILDING ONE OF THE WORLD'S LARGEST INTERIOR FURNISHINGS COMPANIES. HE FOUNDED INTERFACE IN 1973. RAY AND HIS COMPANY REVOLUTIONIZED THE COMMERCIAL FLOOR COVERING INDUSTRY BY PRODUCING AMERICA'S FIRST FREE-LAY CARPET TILES. NOW, RAY HAS EMBARKED ON A MISSION TO "BE THE FIRST COMPANY THAT, BY ITS DEEDS, SHOWS THE ENTIRE INDUSTRIAL WORLD WHAT SUSTAINABILITY IS IN ALL ITS DIMENSIONS: PEOPLE, PROCESS, PRODUCT, PLACE, AND PROFITS BY 2020," AND IN DOING SO, TO BECOME RESTORATIVE THROUGH THE POWER OF INFLUENCE. HE'S LEADING A WORLDWIDE EFFORT TO PIONEER THE PROCESSES OF SUSTAINABLE DEVELOPMENT.

RAY HOLDS HONORARY DOCTORATES FROM SIX COLLEGES AND UNIVERSITIES.

I am an industrialist, some would say a radical industrialist, but you can be sure that I am as competitive and as profit minded as anyone you know. My world is the world of business and industry—the technosphere, if you will—a world where amazing transformation is happening. I would like to draw you into that world, to give you a taste of what it is like as it moves toward sustainability. The example I'm using to illustrate this world is a carpet factory in Georgia, the manager of which is determined to find a sustainable way to design, dye, and produce carpet.

The head of design at the carpet factory gives his design team an outrageous assignment: to go into the forest and see how nature would design a floor covering. "And don't come back with leaf designs; that's not what I mean. Come back

with nature's design principles." The head of design has read BIOMIMICRY, by Janine Benyus. (BIOMIMICRY: nature as teacher, nature as inspiration, nature as mentor and measure.)

So the design team spends a day studying the forest floor and the stream beds, and they come to realize there is total diversity, even chaos—no two things are alike, no two sticks, no two stones, no two leaves. Yet there is a very pleasant orderliness in this chaos. So the designers go back to the design studio and design a carpet tile such that the face designs of no two tiles are identical. All are similar, but every one is different, contrary to the prevailing industrial paradigm that every mass-produced item must be the "cookie-cutter" same, reflecting our traditional predilection for man-made perfection.

This new product is introduced to the market with the name "Entropy" (meaning "disorder"), and in a year and a half it moves to the top of the factory's best-seller list, faster than any other product ever has. The advantages of breaking the old paradigm, insistence on perfection and sameness, are surprisingly numerous: there is almost no waste and no off-quality in production. Inspectors cannot find defects among the deliberate "imperfection" of no-two-alike. The installer can install tiles very quickly, without having to take the traditional care to get the pile nap running uniformly—the less uniform the installation, the better; so he can just take tiles out of the box the way they come and lay them randomly. There is almost no scrap during installation; even piece-tiles can find a place.

Yet, even with these unexpected benefits, is there still more to explain the success of "Entropy"? Perhaps there is. A speaker on the environmental speaking circuit begins every speech by having her audience close their eyes and picture that ideal place of peace, repose, serenity, creativity, comfort, and security—that perfect comfort zone. Then she asks, "How many were somewhere indoors?" And almost no one ever raises a hand. We humans seem to gravitate to nature for that ideal comfort zone. Somehow, perhaps Entropy brings outdoors indoors in a subliminal way, and that is its real appeal. This quality has a name: "biophilia." There is enormous power in biomimicry and in biophilia. This is very new thinking. Nature, the inspiration, is by the way anything but uniformly perfect, yet she is very effective!

This is sustainability in action.

Believe me, I could go on and on with examples of new thinking. Eleven years of this kind of new thinking and innovation, combined with a determination to abandon the comfort of the status quo, can produce unimagined results. Yet it does not come naturally, only through extraordinary commitment. The status quo is a powerful opiate, is it not? Breaking institutional inertia, "We've always done it this way," is hard. Yet, I do know an industrial company that did make the break in the total, absolute, wholehearted pursuit of sustainability and in the process is completely trans-forming itself.

Consequently, I can report to you today that this company, which was once so petro-intensive for its energy and raw materials you could have said it was an extension of the petrochemical industry, has, from that starting place with the new thinking I just described and a sense of shared purpose, over the last ten years, reduced its global net greenhouse gas emissions by 60 percent in absolute tonnage against its 1996 baseline. (For comparison, the Kyoto treaty, which the U.S. refuses to ratify, calls for 7 percent reduction by 2012.)

This company reckons it has reduced its overall environmental footprint by more than 40 percent and, by the year 2020,

believes it will be sustainable, with zero environmental footprint: taking nothing from earth that is not rapidly and naturally renewable (not another fresh drop of oil) and doing no harm to the biosphere.

This company's people will tell you emphatically that these initiatives have been amazingly good for business. Its costs are down, not up, dispelling a myth and exposing the false choice between economy and environment. Its products are the best they have ever been, because sustainable design has provided an unexpected wellspring of innovation. Its people are galvanized around a shared higher purpose. You cannot beat this for bringing people together. Better people are applying, and the best people are staying and working with purpose. And the goodwill in the marketplace generated by this initiative exceeds, by far, what any amount of advertising or marketing expenditure could have generated.

I know this company very well because it is my company, Interface, and I know firsthand that everything I just said about it is true. I also know it could not have happened or continue to happen without the support of our customers.

In the summer of 1994, at age sixty, in the twenty-second year of the company I founded from scratch in 1973, I read Paul Hawken's book, THE ECOLOGY OF COMMERCE; it changed my life and my view of the world. It came for me at a propitious moment. Our customers, especially interior designers, had begun to ask a question we had not heard before, "What is Interface doing for the environment?" So I had agreed, reluctantly, to speak to a newly assembled environmental task force of Interface people from around the world. I had been asked to provide them with my environmental vision, a vision I did not have, and to address this awkward question, "What are you doing . . . ?" Awkward for me, because I could not get beyond, "We obey the law; we comply"; and somehow I knew that "comply" was not a vision.

Hawken's book changed everything for me. I read it, I got it, and I committed this third child of mine (after my two natural daughters) to the path to sustainability.

This new business paradigm has a name: doing well by doing good—cause and effect, effect and cause, all rolled into one positive feedback loop that is good for the earth. This is how the triple bottom line of corporate social responsibility—economy, environment, social equity—done right, will come together in one truly superior, ethical, honest, and legitimate financial bottom line, and companies everywhere will want to emulate the example. And that is how an entire industrial system can move toward sustainability.

I see no other long-term choice for the entire industrial system if it is to survive. Not just our industry, all industry, has got to make this transition, undergo this transformation to survive. Those who don't, won't.

Ray C. Anderson

TACHI KIUCHI
CHAIRMAN FUTURE 500

AS CHAIRMAN AND CEO OF MITSUBISHI ELECTRIC AMERICA, TACHI KIUCHI BUILT THE MITSUBISHI ELECTRIC BRAND IN THE U.S. AND MANAGED THE COMPANY'S TRANSITION FROM THE OLD TO THE NEW ECONOMY. AS MANAGING DIRECTOR OF MITSUBISHI ELECTRIC CORPORATION, HE BROKE WITH JAPANESE CORPORATE NORMS TO CHAMPION A "LIVING SYSTEMS" APPROACH TO BUSINESS THAT INCLUDED RAPID ADAPTATION, FINANCIAL TRANSPARENCY, OPENNESS, CULTURAL DIVERSITY, AND ENVIRONMENTAL SUSTAINABILITY. HE EVEN FORGED A BOLD AGREEMENT WITH RAINFOREST ACTION NETWORK (RAN) TO PROMOTE CORPORATE SUSTAINABILITY.

TODAY, AS CHAIRMAN OF FUTURE 500, AND CEO OF TOKYO-BASED E-SQUARE, KIUCHI INFORMS AND INSPIRES BUSINESS LEADERS ALL OVER THE WORLD AND DEVELOPS PROFITABLE AND SUSTAINABLE BUSINESS PRACTICES AT COMPUTER, ELECTRONICS, AUTOMOBILE, AND OTHER COMPANIES. HE IS THE COAUTHOR, WITH BILL SHIREMAN, OF THE POPULAR BOOK **WHAT WE LEARNED IN THE RAINFOREST: BUSINESS LESSONS FROM NATURE**, WHICH DECLARES THE BUSINESS-AS-MACHINE ERA OVER, AND SHOWS HOW COMPANIES CAN BECOME AS INNOVATIVE AS THE RAINFOREST, LEVERAGING FEEDBACK TO GROW MORE PROFITABLE AND SUSTAINABLE THAN EVER.

MESSAGE FROM THE RAINFOREST
In the rainforest,
where the soil is thin, minerals are scarce,
and resources are always in short supply,
life is extraordinarily rich, more abundant and diverse than
anywhere else on earth.

There is a simmering dynamism in the forest, as organisms
constantly chase the increments of sunlight, water, and
minerals that are always at a premium.

Yet through all their interplay with one another,
the plants and animals of the rainforest find the unique niches,
places where they fit better than any others,
where their specialized forms make them masters of skill and
efficiency,
using just what they need of the scarce resources that are
delivered to them,
"just in time," as those resources cascade through multiple
stages of recycling.

Limits are a constant reality in the rainforest,
yet, paradoxically, scarcity is its own remedy.
It triggers constant feedback, learning, and adaptations that
shape the organisms
and the relationships between organisms so that an
extraordinary richness of life is created.

On a constant flow of energy from the sun, resources recycle
continuously from the earth,
and nothing else but a complex and ever-changing design,
life, flourishes in the rainforest in more concentrated
abundance than anywhere else on the planet.

Sometimes life departs from the rainforest for a time, only to
return there later,
for lessons that can be learned only at home.

We return there now.

Tachi Kiuchi

PETER PRICE-THOMAS,
DEPUTY DIRECTOR OF THE NATURAL STEP U.K.

PETER PRICE-THOMAS WORKS FOR AN INTERNATIONAL SUSTAINABLE DEVELOPMENT ORGANIZATION THE NATURAL STEP (TNS), OF WHICH FORUM FOR THE FUTURE IS THE U.K. LICENSE HOLDER. PETER WORKS WITH FORUM BUSINESS PARTNERS AND THE WIDER CORPORATE SECTOR—USING THE NATURAL STEP'S APPROACH—TO HELP THEM STRATEGICALLY ADDRESS ISSUES OF SUSTAINABILITY. BEFORE JOINING THE FORUM, PETER WAS THE DIRECTOR OF EDUCATIONAL DEVELOPMENT FOR TNS U.S. HE HAS WORKED ON SUSTAINABILITY ISSUES IN NORTH AMERICA, EUROPE, AND ASIA—INCLUDING WORK WITH CORPORA-TIONS, STATE AND NATIONAL GOVERNMENTS, EDUCATIONAL INSTITUTIONS, AND MULTILATERAL AGENCIES. PETER IS A FULBRIGHT SCHOLAR, AND HAS A MASTER'S DEGREE IN ENVIRONMENTAL SCIENCE FROM YALE UNIVERSITY AND AN M.A. IN GEOGRAPHY FROM THE UNIVERSITY OF EDINBURGH.

It is often said that the most sustainable building is the one that is never built: one that does not take any land, nor use any materials; a building that does not use any energy, nor create any waste. And yet, this building is unsustainable in one key aspect: it does not provide for human need. The basic human need of shelter has been with us for millennia and will continue to be with us as long as human life on this planet exists. It is a need not only for some, but for all, and a view of sustainability that does not cater for these needs is far from sustainable.

In these times of increasing global population and consumption it is tempting to try to protect areas from development, to cordon them off for conservation, to say, "We mustn't use any more resources." But humans whose needs are not met are no respecters of such arbitrary limits. No longer can we carry on with business as usual in one place and seek solely to "offset" our negative impacts by setting aside another. Rather, we should seek to develop in such a way that is restorative to the social and natural systems that surround us. Only when we have maximized the positive impact of our development and minimized the negative should we seek to "pay the balance" by offsetting elsewhere.

So how, then, does one go about building in a restorative manner? Firstly, identify the need or service that is to be met, be it one of shelter for a house, or education for a school, or patient health in a hospital. Then envision what success would look like. How could you provide that service in such a way as not to overwhelm nature or society? Design the service provision in such a way that it maximizes the positive and reduces the negative? Do you actually need to build a structure to achieve it? If you do, design it with the end of use in mind, so that all the materials can be readily reused; build on a plot that has already been taken from nature, with materials that aren't virgin; power the building using free distributed energy from the sun or wind; insulate well; and, most of all, always think of the service that is being provided.

Over the next fifty years the world's population will increase one-and-a-half-fold. Over the same time, consumption per capita will go up between four- and six-fold. People's needs, including that of shelter, have to be met, and yet the natural systems upon which we are dependent are already in significant decline. How, then, are we to have any hope of meeting these needs? Einstein once suggested, "We cannot solve our problems with the thinking we used when we created them." In order to achieve sustainability in buildings we need a fundamental shift in thinking—from creating buildings to providing for human need. And to do this we need to build restoratively.

Peter Price-Thomas

EDWIN DATSCHEFSKI,
FOUNDER OF BIOTHINKING INTERNATIONAL

EDWIN DATSCHEFSKI HELPS PEOPLE FIGURE OUT HOW TO MAKE THEIR PRODUCTS SUSTAINABLE: GOOD FOR PEOPLE, PROFITS, AND THE PLANET. HE IS THE AUTHOR OF **TOTAL BEAUTY OF SUSTAINABLE DESIGN,** WHICH IS USED BY MOST DESIGN SCHOOLS AND DESIGNERS AS A REFERENCE AND GUIDE ON SUSTAINABLE PRODUCT DESIGN. EDWIN DEVELOPED THE CYCLIC/SOLAR/SAFE METHODOLOGY FOR ASSESSING THE ENVIRONMENTAL PERFORMANCE OF PRODUCTS AND PROCESSES.

EDWIN'S BACKGROUND IS AS A BIOLOGIST AT BRISTOL UNIVERSITY. AFTER WORKING IN THE AEROSPACE INDUSTRY HE SPENT EIGHT YEARS WORKING AT THE ENVIRONMENT COUNCIL, DEVELOPING PROGRAMS INVOLVING THOUSANDS OF U.K. BUSINESSES TO ENABLE THEM TO REALIZE THE BENEFITS OF IMPROVED ENVIRONMENTAL PERFORMANCE. EDWIN HAS TRAINED OVER 6,000 PEOPLE IN ENVIRONMENTAL MANAGEMENT AND SUSTAINABLE PRODUCT DESIGN. AS PART OF HIS PERSONAL EDUCATIONAL MISSION, EDWIN HAS ALSO DEVELOPED A SET OF FREE WEB-BASED EDUCATIONAL RESOURCES FOR PEOPLE TO USE TO LEARN ABOUT SUSTAINABLE DESIGN.
Visit www.biothinking.com.

Every day each of us changes the world. We change it primarily through the side effects of the physical trans-formation of materials that make up the products, energy, and food we consume. Unfortunately this change is almost always detrimental, as even products that seem beautiful on the outside have a hidden ugliness behind them, an ugliness caused by exploitation of workers, releases of pollution, and destruction of habitats. The world is so fundamentally wrong when it comes to the way products are designed and made that it is hard to comprehend.

In a strange kind of blessing, these horrors below the surface are starting to manifest themselves in ways even the most thick-skinned skeptics can no longer deny, and this has spurred many nations and businesses to radically improve their products and industrial and agricultural processes. Yet there is still a huge mountain of product types, perhaps hundreds of millions, that need to be redesigned to be properly compatible with nature.

Martin Hill's work shows how, in a very pure way, materials can be borrowed from nature to make a physical product that performs a function or service—in this case the stirring of people's souls. Unlike traditional artists' materials, when the materials Martin has used are returned to nature, they continue on their geological or organic pathways, and the cycles of life are unbroken.

Can we achieve similar purity in the design and manufacture of everyday products? This is the simple goal. Instead of using pigments and oils, Martin uses leaves and stones, and so in an analogous way mass-produced products can be designed to be cyclic at a molecular level, able to be consumed in turn by recycling machines or composted by microorganisms and rebuilt with no persistent wastes into new materials and new products once more.

All products are ultimately as ephemeral as a leaf. The average household object has a useful life of only a few months. So it needs to be as easily assimilated back into the system as a leaf is. From earth, to earth, to earth . . .

This is not just about the obvious things like recycled paper or recyclable packaging. We now have the techniques and technologies to make it easy for people to design or redesign any product at all and make it better, from barbecues and binoculars to suitcases and swimming goggles, from cars and lipstick to ocean liners and sushi.

There has been such a dilution of the term "sustainability" that it seems even a slight benefit to the community or a modest saving in energy use gets described as sustainable. Instead we need to think about becoming 100 percent sustainable on an absolute level; a threshold which we are as yet far from attaining but one that is theoretically and practicably achievable in our own lifetime.

One hundred percent sustainable products are renewable, efficient, and fair. This means totally renewable (cyclic, solar, and safe) and superefficient in their use of materials and energy. It means fair to humans in the form of workers, neighbors, shareholders, and consumers. But also, as has been too often overlooked, fair to nonhumans. We need to be fairer to the wildlife and all the species of plants and animals whose habitats we are trampling in our blind rush to extract materials.

In the twenty-first century we must recognize that becoming 100 percent sustainable is not only possible but required. We will not achieve this while there is still the widely held misconception that sustainability is optional or that it is some kind of moral behavior that requires unilateral individual sacrifice in favor of the environment.

Humans and nonhumans are part of the same system, so when we harm nature we are committing self-harm as surely as a razor blade on our own arms.

Deep within each of us is the feeling that we are part of a larger whole, and that the everyday, institutionalized violation of nature to bring us our daily needs is profoundly wrong. By taking one of our purest emotions, the appreciation of art and beauty, we can begin to assuage those feelings and through this book begin to understand the path to true sustainability that lies before us.

Edwin Datschefski

BEHIND THE
WORK

Seeing the photographs of these sculptures collected together in this book reminds me vividly of the experience of making them.

Some stand out because they were so spontaneous, even instantaneous: a fleeting shaft of sunlight glimpsed through a rock crevice, a chance finding such as a thin sheet of ice on a pond in a valley that the sun hadn't yet reached.

Others truly tested our perseverance: the wind rearranging leaves or feathers that we'd patiently placed, just as the shot was ready; and our stamina: standing for long periods in very cold water; and our resourcefulness in isolated locations: getting down from a climb in near darkness after waiting for just the right light to take a photograph.

Of course behind the scenes there were some sculptures that were not so successful, but even so they were an experience, and each time what was learned would be valuable for the next.

As a designer all his life—a designer specializing in visual communications—Martin has a trained eye. Qualities such as composition, texture, and contrast, as well as color and light, are his language.

My contribution varied: sometimes my practical skills were called upon; other times a sharp eye for collecting materials was helpful; sometimes Martin worked alone. But always the image of the sculpture was pre-visualized by him and this body of work is an expression of his philosophy.

Many of the sculptures were made during our travels, such as Pine Needle Infinity on the granite domes we climbed in Southern California, Floating Frond Circle in Madagascar, and Maple Leaf Arch over a mossy stream near a shrine in Japan.

Others, however, were created at places that we know well and where we spent a lot of time. The ignimbrite cliffs of Whanganui Bay in the North Island of New Zealand were a magnet for us and our climbing friends from all over the world. Over the years we returned there to pitch our tent for days of climbing in the sun high up on the cliffs—watching the trout swimming in the deep, clear water of Lake Taupo below; in the evenings relaxing and cooking round a fire with our friends.

Because we were camping we had time. Martin could wait for the warm low angle light of dusk or dawn, a full moon, or the even light of an overcast day. A sculpture made at dusk could be left overnight to be photographed in the early morning from a different angle. The sculpture could also be observed dispersing naturally, which felt right to us as the cycle was completed.

The shallow lagoon of water where the Whanganui stream flowed into the lake was an inspiration for sculptures that featured the reflective qualities of still water. Each time we were there the lagoon would be configured differently according to the flow of the stream, the wind, or the rain, and this stimulated fresh ideas.

After storms pumice stones would wash up on the beach, itself consisting of sand made from finely worn-down pumice pebbles.

Years later we would still find stones with holes in them from the making of the Stone Circle sculpture. After floating away they would have eventually become waterlogged and sunk, only to be washed up again in another storm somewhere on the lakeshore. It gave us a feeling of continuity.

This sense of process was even more graphic, for us, in Climbing Sculpture, which was made on top of a climb called Tibia at Whanganui Bay. It involved taking sand from the beach with us on our climb up the cleft behind the pinnacle to the

top. Other climbers got accustomed to seeing the sand there until it washed away in the rain, returning to the beach. Later a re-creation of this sculpture made with a two-man television crew—a presenter and a camera/sound man—became an adventure for the presenter who needed to talk to us on the top but struggled to negotiate the terrifyingly steep track back down with me, while his intrepid cameraman rappelled down with Martin, his heavy gear strapped to his back.

The Maori people who belong to this land have their own strong sense of continuity with the place. They enjoy seeing the climbers who visit and understand how much we love it there.

Some sculptures were part of a bigger project, such as those made in the millennium year where we created twelve sculptures each containing 2,000 elements. Sculptures such as 2,000 Floating Stones and 2,000 Berries had us counting carefully, which added another dimension to the preparation of materials.

Materials are only part of the process. Location and the conditions are the other fundamental ingredients. The ideas are expressed by learning from and working with the relationships between these ingredients.

Making the photograph is the final stage for Martin. In choosing the angle he isolates the sculpture from the extraneous or irrelevant things that might distract from it. The quality of light is what brings the image to life in the camera.

Many of the sculptures were created on the wild, empty beaches west of Auckland, the city where we lived until recently. With the black ironsand and rugged bush, it was an ideal solitary escape for Martin as sculpture making became more and more the focus of his workday.

In 2004 we made a commitment of a different kind. We moved to Wanaka in the foothills of New Zealand's Southern Alps. Here we designed and built an energy-efficient house and studio where we live and work surrounded by a natural environment of mountains, glaciers, lakes, forests, rivers, and rock faces.

We realize that to live in this place is a privilege in a world so ravaged and torn by humans in conflict with each other and with nature. But this only serves to strengthen our resolve to work toward the protection of the natural world for all future generations.

Philippa Jones

AFTERWORD

Art is about feeling. Science is about knowing. Design is about possibility.

We still know so little about life and natural systems—species are being destroyed faster than we discover them. The good news is that sustainable solutions for everything are being discovered all over the world by those studying and copying nature's evolved designs.

I came to New Zealand from England out of curiosity more than half my lifetime ago.

I stayed because I found a diversity and vibrancy in the land and the people to which I feel a sense of belonging. Both the land and the culture are young and this makes for a feeling of freedom and possibility.

It is because of this strong sense of the possible in New Zealand that I was able to eventually throw off the self-protective urge to continue running a normal design business and follow the uncertain path of environmental artist and sustainable designer.

To me designing a sustainable way to live is the biggest project on earth and I believe the answers are to be found in nature's designs. So I am especially grateful to the authors of the essays in EARTH TO EARTH whose collaborative spirit, wisdom, and insights surely form the framework on which our sustainable future will be built.

I am not a scientist but I have always felt a deep connection with and a need to try and understand the natural world. The deepest connections for me come from being in direct contact with the elements of the earth: rock, water, leaves, ice. It is only through working with and learning from the inter-connected and interdependent cyclic forces within nature that I have found a way to express myself fully.

I could only have done this with the support and encouragement of the many people who are included in the acknowledgments at the end of this book. But my deepest love and thanks must go to my partner, Philippa Jones, with whom I have shared experiences, good and bad, on the great journey of the past thirteen years. Her love, support, and collaboration, often in the face of adversity, has been a great source of joy to me. Her contribution to this body of work has been immense.

I would also like to thank my parents, Ronald and Olive Hill, now sadly deceased; they would have loved to see this book. They instilled in me the values I hold to this day and without which I would be lost.

Martin Hill

AFTERWORD

Many people ask us about the making of the sculptures: How did you do that? How long did it take? Where did the idea come from? And even Which one do you like the most?

There is, in fact, one that is significant to me, a previously unpublished one. It is our hands imprinted on rock and it signifies my commitment to Martin.

Climbing brought us together. We met in 1994, when we were both exploring a fresh approach to life—Martin was returning to rock climbing after fifteen years away from it and I was discovering rock climbing as a way to embrace challenge and adventure. We both wanted to explore hard-to-get-to places.

Hand Print Sculpture was made on the top of a granite pinnacle called the Cathedral on Mt. Buffalo, Victoria, Australia. After climbing the cracks to the top, Martin leading with the rope and me following, we were able to clip our harnesses into the fixed anchor placed there by climbers long before us for the purpose of rappelling off.

The sloping top was about the size of a large dining room table—there was just enough room to move around. The low light of evening was beautiful for photographing a sculpture but our only material on the bare granite was lichen. We scraped off enough with a carabiner, the only tool we had, to sprinkle over our hands pressed onto the rock.

The imprint would last only until the next breeze blew it away, but the idea that it expresses—of working together harmoniously—remains. The photograph still speaks to me of the beginning of our life together, at first as climbing partners (which by its very nature required good communication skills, trust, faith in each other's ability, and awareness of each other's strengths and weaknesses) and then as a couple, living and working and laughing together.

The small contribution I made to the realization of the sculptures in this book has enriched my life. As has Martin.

Philippa Jones

DIRECTORY

MOUNTAIN STONES
Volcanic rocks, moss, herbs, and alpine flowers photographed between rainstorms.

AMBER MOUNTAIN CIRCLE
Leaves and dense ferns in tropical rainforest.

LACE LEAF CIRCLE 2
Partially decayed mahoe leaves floated on pond.

FROST BRACKEN CIRCLE
Bracken leaves on thick-frost-covered rock.

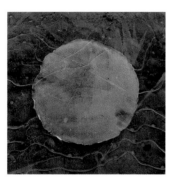

MATUKITUKI ICE DISC
Thin sheet of ice on frozen pool.

SHELL SPIRAL
Seashells on black ironsand beach.

PUMICE RING
Carved pumice stone on lakeside pumice beach.

HOKKAIDO ROCK CIRCLE
Volcanic stones on moss near volcano summit.

HEATHER CIRCLE
Circle of heather in Scottish glen.

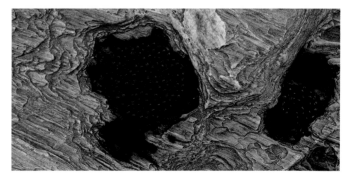

RED BERRY CIRCLES
Hawthorn berries on water-eroded rock.

DRY SEASON CIRCLE
Orange-lichen-covered stones on fragile surface of cracked mud in wetlands.

POHUTUKAWA LEAF CIRCLE
Fallen pohutukawa leaves on ironsand beach.

2,000 BERRIES
Coprosma berries gathered, counted, and carried to rock ledge above lake.

EUCALYPTUS LEAF LINE
Eucalyptus leaves arranged on fallen lakeside tree at sunset.

RIVER STONE AND PETALS
Wet wildflower petals stuck to river stone.

SPLIT CIRCLE
Colored stones arranged over windblasted rock on sand dunes.

GORGE CIRCLE
Autumn leaves floated on rock pool in river gorge.

KANUKA CIRCLE
Dried kanuka branches placed in lake bed to catch early morning reflection.

AUTUMN LEAF CIRCLE
Fallen leaves removed from riverbank and floated in eddy to complete circle.

SUN CIRCLE
Ram's horn shells on ironsand beach at sunset.

CLAY CIRCLES
Circles of lake-bed clay placed on alpine-river rock at dusk.

FLOATING FROND CIRCLE
Intertwined branches floating over rock in mountain stream.

GREEN LEAF CIRCLE
Leaves fixed to thorny branch reflected in lagoon.

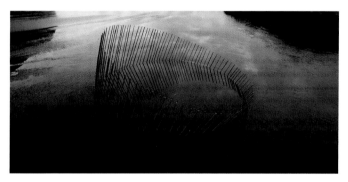

RISING CIRCLE
Sticks inserted into wet sand in rising tide.

KANUKA SPHERE
Intertwined dried kanuka branches reflected in calm lake.

STREAM STONE CIRCLE
Sea-worn stones at sunset placed where small stream meets sea.

SPRING CIRCLE
Wildflowers fixed in cracks of weathered lakeshore tree trunk.

LACE LEAF CIRCLE 1
Partially decayed mahoe leaves floated on stream to briefly form small circle.

MEADOW CIRCLE
Wildflowers placed in grass in memory of my mother, Olive Hill.

KOWHAI FLOWER LINE
Fallen kowhai flowers arranged in split tree branch.

EUCALYPTUS LEAF CIRCLE
Fallen eucalyptus leaves on high rock plateau.

WEATHERED STONES
Water-worn stones on weathered alpine-lake rock.

GRASS SPHERE WANAKA
Dune-grass sphere placed lakeside.

STANDING CIRCLE
Carved pumice stone balanced beside lake.

FEATHER CIRCLE
Seabird feathers inserted into sand at dusk.

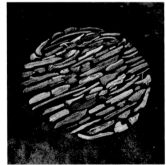

DRIFTWOOD CIRCLE
Driftwood arranged on lakeshore.

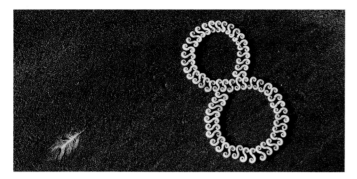

SHELL INFINITY
Ram's horn shells forming infinity symbol on beach.

CIRCLE OF CIRCLES
Flax circles held together with thorns and flax strands.

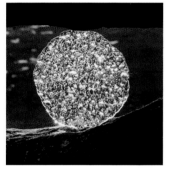

ROCK AND ICE CIRCLE
Sheet of ice shaped and balanced in rock formation.

ROYS PEAK SNOW CIRCLE
Springtime snow compressed and carved into circle.

LAKEBED CLAY CIRCLE 1
Lakebed clay carved into circle.

LAKEBED CLAY CIRCLE 2
Lakebed clay carved into circle.

2,000 PINE NEEDLES
Pine needles from forest floor counted and arranged on sand beneath natural rock arch.

GRASS SPHERE 3
Dune grass woven into sphere.

STONE CIRCLE
Volcanic pumice stones threaded on green stick and reflected in calm pond.

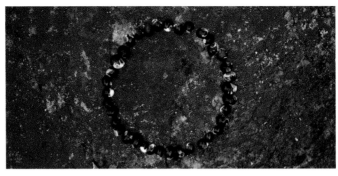

SHELL CIRCLE
Black shells arranged on lichen-covered rock.

TWO STONES
Smooth worn rocks balanced beside lake at sunset.

BALANCED BOULDERS
Boulders balanced on rock by mountain lake.

NINE RED LEAVES
Leaves placed on partly submerged granite river boulder and photographed before being washed away.

KAURI LEAF CIRCLE
Fallen leaves placed on moss by rainforest stream.

GREEN PEBBLE RING
Small green pebbles arranged on rock outcrop by sea.

SNOW CIRCLE
Snow built into circle to frame view of volcano beyond.

SILVER FERN CIRCLE
Fern fronds tied with vines to encircle fallen tree beside rainforest stream.

ORANGE STONES UNDER WATER
Coloured stones placed underwater at lake's edge.

ANAWHATA SPHERE
Grass roots woven into spherical structure on cliffs above surf beach.

2000 CIRCLES
Snow disc left for week then pierced with holes to allow sun to shine through at dawn.

YELLOW LEAF CIRCLE
Floating autumn leaves briefly held in place in still pond.

LEAF CYCLE
Pohutukawa leaves inserted in wet ironsand at water's edge, backlit by sun.

2,000 STONES
Pumice stones collected from lakeshore, counted and corralled into floating circle on pond using sticks under water.

BLACKBERRY LEAF CIRCLE
Decaying blackberry leaves pinned to thorny branch, backlit by sun.

LACE LEAF
Decaying puka leaf on eroded rock.

FLOATING STONES
Pumice stones floating on surface of lake, held in place underwater by sticks.

BEACH CIRCLE
Stones removed from beach to make circle at low tide.

WOVEN TOETOE STICKS
Toetoe sticks woven into upright structure on wet sand.

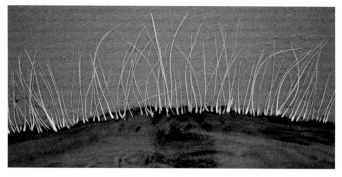

GRASSES
Seed stems from beach grasses laid on edge of stream.

2,000 PETALS
Fallen camellia petals gathered, counted, and laid on sphagnum moss beside boiling thermal spring.

MAPLE LEAF ARCH
Curved stick wrapped with wet maple leaves balanced momentarily across rushing water.

MOUNTAIN STONE CIRCLE
Rounded stones placed on flat lakeside rock.

SNOW INFINITY
Snow shaped into infinity symbol on glacier.

CLIMBING SCULPTURE
Sand collected from lakeshore and carried up rock pinnacle to create sculpture on summit.

2,000 PEBBLES
Beach pebbles collected, counted and arranged on lichen-covered rock.

FLOWING STONES
Stones collected from riverbank to build ridge in fast-flowing water.

PINE NEEDLE INFINITY
Pine needles collected from cracks on summit rocks to make infinity symbol.

ENCIRCLED STONE
Fallen pohutukawa leaves inserted into sand at low tide.

BEACH STONE RINGS
Large round stones on beach with incoming tide.

WOVEN WORLD
Willow woven into half sphere reflected in lake.

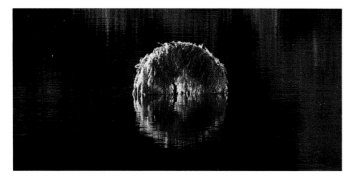

TOETOE SUN
Toetoe seed heads intertwined and reflected in stream to form circle.

TINY ROCK CIRCLE
Small rocks in mountain stream.

WATER CYCLE 3
Sticks cut to size pushed into sand and reflected in tidal pool.

MARTIN WITH BEACH STONE RINGS
Large round stones on beach washed by incoming tide
Image by Ralph Talmont.

HAND PRINT SCULPTURE
Hands placed on rock and sprinkled with lichen to leave imprint.

ACKNOWLEDGMENTS

Many of the sculptures in this book were made in the joyful company of—and often in collaboration with my partner, Philippa Jones, who has also greatly enhanced EARTH TO EARTH through her contribution of text and images. This book is dedicated to her.

I especially thank the contributors to EARTH TO EARTH who donated their time and wisdom to provide their unique vision for a sustainable future: Jonathon Porritt for his introduction; Dr. Karl-Henrik Robèrt for his essay on art in nature; Ray Anderson for his essay on sustainable industry; Tachi Kiuchi for his message from the rainforest; Peter Price-Thomas for his essay on sustainable building; Edwin Datschefski for his essay on sustainable design; and, of course, Sir Edmund Hillary for his foreword.

The sculpture photographs were created over thirteen years in several different countries. I offer grateful thanks to the following people who have supported me or helped in the development of the licensing and publishing of my work during this period: Anne Ackerman, Syd Atkins, Tracey Borgfeldt, Rob Donze, Mark Feenstra, Arno Gasteiger, Len Gillman, Hisae Koyanagi, Brian Richards, David Robinson, Deirdre Robinson, Gus Roxborough, Jun Sato, Judy Shane, and Ralph Talmont.

Special thanks also to the Maori people of Whanganui Bay, Lake Taupo, on whose land we have spent so much time climbing and creating sculptures.

The following companies have been important in achieving the widespread distribution of my images to the public in many parts of the world. I would like to thank them for their support: Image Centre NZ, Image Gallery NZ, Propaganda Publishing NZ, Devon Publishing UK, Portal Publishing UK, The Art Group UK, and Godwit Publishing NZ.

I would like to thank those people who have generously allowed for their comments on the earth's environment to be quoted within this book.

This book would not have happened without the creativity and expertise of the team at PQ Blackwell. Their dedication to outstanding quality and design in publishing has made working with them a great pleasure.

My sincere thanks to all.

Martin Hill

ISBN-13: 978-0-7407-6934-4
ISBN-10: 0-7407-6934-0
Library of Congress Control Number: 2007922166

www.andrewsmcmeel.com

Produced and originated by PQ Blackwell Limited
116 Symonds Street, Auckland, New Zealand
www.pqblackwell.com

The publisher is grateful for literary permissions to reproduce those items below subject to copyright. Every effort has been made to trace the copyright holders and the publisher apologizes for any unintentional omission. We would be pleased to hear from any not acknowledged here and undertake to make all reasonable efforts to include the appropriate acknowledgment in any subsequent editions.

Excerpts from Lost Woods: The Discovered Writing of Rachel Carson, Copyright © 1998 by Roger Allen Christie and The Sea Around Us by Rachel Carson, Copyright © 1950 by Rachel L. Carson used with permission from Frances Collin, Trustee. Excerpt from Biomimicry by Janine M. Benyus, Copyright 1997 by Janine M. Benyus, reprinted by permission of HarperCollins Publishers. Excerpt from A Study of History by Toynbee, Arnold J. (1987), by permission of Oxford University Press Inc. Excerpt from Wabi-Sabi: for Artists, Designers, Poets & Philosophers by Leonard Koren, Copyright © 1994 by Leonard Koren, Stone Bridge Press, reprinted by permission of the author. Excerpt from This Is the American Earth by Nancy Newhall with Ansel Adams, Little, Brown and Company, reprinted by permission. Extract from Aphorisms for Leo Baeck (1952) by Albert Einstein, Albert Einstein Archives. Extract from Ends and Means (1937) by Aldous Huxley, reprinted by permission.

This book is printed on sustainably produced paper, using mineral free inks, and the jacket is finished with an aqueous seal.

Design concept by Cameron Gibb
Additional design by Victoria Skinner

Printed by 1010 Printing International Ltd, China